Under the Asphalt

Jack Donahue

Published by Defenestration Press, 2025.

Table of Contents

"Roads? Where we're going, we don't need roads."

-Dr. Emmett L. Brown

The Unseen Marketplace

When you think of a parking lot, you might imagine a vast expanse of concrete, delineated by faded white lines and dotted with vehicles parked haphazardly or in orderly rows. To many, it's simply a utilitarian space—an area designed to hold cars while people attend to business elsewhere. However, beneath this seemingly mundane surface lies a vibrant, dynamic marketplace. Each parking space is not merely a spot to leave your vehicle; it is a microeconomic unit, a tiny arena where the forces of supply, demand, and human behavior intersect in fascinating and often unexpected ways.

We will dissect the everyday decisions made by drivers, examine the interplay of market forces, and reveal how the simple act of parking can mirror broader societal trends. By the end of this journey, you will begin to see parking lots not as inert by-products of urban planning but as intricate systems that reflect the complexity of modern life.

The Microcosm of a Parking Space

Imagine for a moment the decision process that occurs when you enter a busy parking lot. Your car slows, and you scan the rows of vehicles, weighing your options. Do you choose a spot near the entrance for convenience, even if it means paying a premium or risking a tight squeeze? Or do you opt for a spot further away, where parking may be free or less costly, yet requires a longer walk? This moment of decision, repeated countless times across cities and suburbs worldwide, encapsulates fundamental economic principles.

At its core, a parking space is a scarce resource. In areas where demand is high—such as downtown districts, shopping centers, or event venues—the availability of parking becomes limited. Drivers, acting as rational agents, respond to this scarcity. They factor in the opportunity cost of their time, the convenience of proximity, and even the perceived prestige associated with a particular spot. In doing so, they inadvertently engage in market behavior that mirrors the broader dynamics of supply and demand found in any economic system.

This microcosm is not isolated from the larger economy. The pricing strategies employed by parking lot owners, the design and layout of the lot, and even the cultural attitudes toward driving and parking all interplay in a manner that is reflective of larger societal trends. For instance, in cities where urban sprawl and traffic congestion are significant issues, the value placed on a convenient parking space skyrockets. Conversely, in areas with robust public transportation systems, parking may be viewed as a less critical commodity.

Supply, Demand, and the Value of Convenience

To appreciate parking lots as marketplaces, one must first understand the interplay of supply and demand within them. Supply in this context is straightforward—the number of parking spaces available in a given area. Demand, however, is more complex and is influenced by multiple factors including the time of day, the day of the week, local events, and even weather conditions.

Consider a bustling downtown district during a Friday evening. The demand for parking is not just high because of the sheer number of people arriving, but also because each driver assigns a different value to convenience. Some may be willing to pay a premium to park close to popular restaurants and entertainment venues, while others might prefer to endure a longer walk to save money. This differentiation in preferences creates a tiered market within the parking lot itself, where price and location signal quality and convenience.

Parking lot operators, in response, employ various pricing strategies to manage demand. Dynamic pricing, much like what is used in airline tickets or ride-sharing services, adjusts the cost of parking based on real-time factors. During peak hours, prices may surge to reflect the high demand, while during off-peak times, they might drop to attract customers. This system not only maximizes revenue but also serves as an economic signal to drivers, guiding their decisions about when and where to park.

The convenience factor extends beyond mere proximity. Safety, lighting, and the perceived security of a location also contribute to the overall value of a parking space. A well-lit, monitored parking lot in a safe neighborhood might command higher prices compared to an isolated, poorly maintained lot. These factors, though intangible, are critical components of the economic calculus that drivers perform, often subconsciously, when selecting a parking spot.

The Psychology Behind Parking Decisions

Beyond the clear-cut economic considerations of supply and demand, there is a rich tapestry of human psychology at work in parking decisions. Behavioral economics teaches us that people do not always act as perfectly rational agents. Instead, their choices are often influenced by biases, heuristics, and social cues.

One fascinating phenomenon is the concept of "loss aversion." Drivers might prefer a spot near the entrance not just for convenience, but also to avoid the potential loss of time and energy that comes with a longer walk. This preference persists even when the actual difference in walking distance is negligible, highlighting how the anticipation of loss (in this case, wasted time) can outweigh the potential gain from saving money.

Another psychological factor is the "endowment effect." Once a driver has secured a parking spot, they may overvalue it simply because it is theirs. This can lead to a reluctance to move to a potentially better spot if it becomes available later, reflecting a deep-seated bias where individuals place a higher value on what they already possess.

Social influences also play a significant role. In crowded urban settings, the act of parking can become a subtle competition. The way a car is parked—its alignment within the space, the ease with which a driver can navigate out—can signal social status, attention to detail, or even personal discipline. Such behaviors are not merely about utility; they are imbued with cultural significance that speaks to broader societal values and norms.

Moreover, the layout and design of the parking lot itself can subtly influence behavior. For example, angled parking spots may encourage drivers to orient their vehicles in a way that maximizes visibility and ease of exit, which in turn can foster a sense of security and order. These design choices, while seemingly trivial, have far-reaching implications for how drivers interact with their environment and with one another.

Parking as an Economic Indicator

Parking lots offer more than just a place to park; they are a barometer for urban health and economic vitality. The availability and pricing of parking spaces can reflect broader trends in economic activity. In thriving economic centers, high demand for parking is often a byproduct of bustling commerce, vibrant nightlife, and a steady influx of tourists. Conversely, in areas experiencing economic downturns, the abundance of empty parking spots can serve as a stark visual indicator of reduced activity and consumer confidence.

Urban planners and economists alike have long recognized the value of parking data in understanding urban dynamics. By analyzing patterns in parking occupancy, pricing fluctuations, and even the time vehicles spend parked, researchers can gain insights into traffic flow, peak business hours, and the overall economic pulse of a region. This data, when integrated with other metrics such as public transit usage and road congestion, helps city officials make informed decisions about infrastructure investments, zoning laws, and urban development strategies.

For instance, consider a city undergoing rapid development. A sudden spike in parking demand might signal that new businesses and residential complexes are drawing people to the area. City planners could use this information to justify the expansion of public transit networks or the creation of additional public spaces. Conversely, a consistent surplus of vacant parking spots might prompt a reevaluation of zoning policies or indicate the need for economic revitalization efforts.

The economic signals emanating from parking lots are not confined to urban centers. In suburban and rural areas, the availability of parking can provide clues about local economic trends. A bustling shopping center with a fully occupied parking lot on weekends may indicate a strong local economy and a thriving community, while a nearly empty lot could suggest underlying issues such as population decline or economic stagnation.

Cultural Codes and the Hidden Language of Parking

Parking is not only an economic transaction; it is also a social and cultural ritual. The choices we make about where and how to park are laden with symbolic meaning, revealing underlying cultural codes that govern our behavior. In many ways, parking lots function as a stage upon which broader cultural narratives play out.

Take, for example, the phenomenon of "prime" parking spots. In many parking lots, certain spaces—often those closest to the entrance or the main building—are highly coveted. These spots are not merely convenient; they are imbued with a sense of status and privilege. Occupying such a space can be seen as a subtle assertion of social standing, a way of signaling one's importance or success without uttering a word. This behavior reflects a broader cultural preoccupation with status symbols and the social hierarchy, where even a parking space becomes a marker of identity and worth.

Similarly, the act of circling a lot in search of that elusive perfect spot can be interpreted as a ritualistic behavior, one that mirrors the human desire for control and mastery over one's environment. This behavior is not random; it is a carefully calculated dance, informed by personal habits, prior experiences, and even the observed behaviors of others. In this sense, every decision made in a parking lot is part of a larger social script, one that encapsulates the interplay of individual desires and collective norms.

Furthermore, the very design of a parking lot—the arrangement of spaces, the flow of traffic, the placement of barriers—can communicate subtle messages about community values and priorities. A parking lot designed with ample green spaces, for instance, may signal a commitment to environmental sustainability, while a lot with high security features might reflect a community's emphasis on safety and order. These design elements, often overlooked, serve as a visual language that communicates much about the ethos of a place.

Case Studies: Real-World Examples of Parking Marketplaces

To truly understand the unseen marketplace of parking, it helps to examine real-world examples where the economic principles we have discussed are vividly on display.

Urban Downtowns

In many major cities around the world, downtown areas represent the epicenter of economic activity. Here, parking is at a premium. Take, for instance, the bustling financial district of a global metropolis. During peak business hours, the demand for parking is so high that even a few minutes of extra walking distance can translate into a significant economic cost. Companies often invest in private parking structures or negotiated parking arrangements to ensure their employees have convenient access to their offices. This phenomenon underscores how parking spaces, as scarce resources, become a commodity whose value is directly linked to time and convenience.

Shopping Malls and Entertainment Centers

Large shopping centers and entertainment venues also serve as microcosms of parking economics. During holiday seasons or major events, the influx of visitors creates a temporary surge in demand that is often met with dynamic pricing strategies. Some malls have experimented with real-time pricing, where the cost of parking fluctuates based on the number of available spaces and the time of day. This not only maximizes revenue for the property owners but also provides consumers with a transparent view of the cost of convenience. In such settings, the act of parking becomes a negotiation between price and accessibility, with each driver weighing the benefits of proximity against the cost incurred.

Suburban and Residential Areas

Even in suburban neighborhoods, where parking might seem less of a concern, the economic dynamics are at play. In residential complexes or gated communities, parking spaces are often allocated based on a combination of availability and perceived value. Some communities have begun to treat parking as a tradable asset, where reserved spaces are bought, sold, or leased among residents. This practice reflects a sophisticated understanding of parking as an economic resource—a commodity that, under the right conditions, can appreciate in value much like real estate itself.

Special Events and Temporary Markets

Consider the phenomenon of parking during major sporting events or concerts. In these scenarios, the demand for parking can skyrocket, turning an ordinary parking lot into a bustling, temporary marketplace. Opportunistic vendors and parking lot owners may implement surge pricing, and drivers are forced to make rapid decisions based on fluctuating costs and availability. These temporary markets offer a concentrated view of how supply and demand can shift dramatically over a short period, highlighting the responsiveness of parking economics to external stimuli.

The Role of Technology in Shaping Parking Behavior

In recent years, technology has begun to revolutionize the way we interact with parking. Innovations such as mobile payment systems, real-time occupancy sensors, and automated parking solutions have added new layers of complexity—and opportunity—to the parking marketplace.

Mobile apps now allow drivers to reserve parking spots in advance, compare prices in real-time, and even receive notifications about available spaces as they approach their destination. This technological integration transforms parking from a reactive experience—where drivers circle aimlessly in search of a spot—into a proactive and optimized decision-making process. The data collected from these apps further enriches our understanding of parking behavior, providing insights into patterns and trends that were previously invisible.

For example, sensor data can reveal how long vehicles typically remain parked in a particular lot, what times of day see the highest turnover, and even how weather conditions impact parking decisions. This information not only benefits individual drivers but also informs urban planners and economists who seek to understand and improve the overall efficiency of urban infrastructure.

Automated parking systems, though still in their nascent stages, promise to further blur the line between technology and traditional economic models. In such systems, vehicles are parked and retrieved by automated machines, reducing the need for human intervention and potentially increasing the density of vehicles in a given space. This technological evolution poses interesting questions about the future of parking as an economic entity. Will the convenience and efficiency of automated systems lead to new pricing models? How will the reduction in human error and variability impact the overall market dynamics? These are questions that researchers and urban planners are only beginning to explore.

Parking as a Mirror of Societal Trends

When we zoom out from the individual parking space to the broader landscape, it becomes clear that parking behavior mirrors larger societal trends. Urban sprawl, the evolution of consumer habits, environmental concerns, and even shifts in work culture (such as the rise of remote work) all influence how we value and use parking spaces.

Urban Sprawl and Density

The design and availability of parking are deeply intertwined with urban planning decisions. In sprawling cities, the abundance of parking spaces often correlates with a car-centric lifestyle, where personal vehicles are not just a means of transportation but a symbol of individual freedom. Conversely, in denser, more walkable urban environments, the scarcity of parking can encourage alternative forms of transportation such as public transit, biking, or walking. This dynamic illustrates how the physical and economic constraints of parking can drive broader changes in transportation habits and urban development.

Environmental Considerations

In an era of increasing environmental awareness, the economics of parking are also evolving in response to ecological concerns. Cities around the world are experimenting with measures to reduce carbon emissions by discouraging car use and promoting sustainable alternatives. Some municipalities have implemented policies that reduce parking availability or increase parking fees in central areas to encourage the use of public transportation. These initiatives not only reflect a commitment to environmental sustainability but also underscore the economic principle that pricing can be used as a tool to shape behavior. By making parking more expensive or less convenient, cities can indirectly promote greener modes of transportation—a testament to the power of economic signals in effecting social change.

The Changing Nature of Work

The COVID-19 pandemic and the subsequent rise of remote work have also left an indelible mark on parking economics. With fewer people commuting to centralized office spaces, many urban parking lots have experienced a decline in demand. This shift has forced property owners and city planners to reconsider the design and allocation of parking spaces. In some cases, former parking areas are being repurposed into public parks, community gardens, or even housing—transformations that reflect a broader societal reevaluation of space in the post-pandemic world. Such changes highlight the fluidity of economic value, where a parking space, once seen solely as a commercial commodity, can become a catalyst for broader social and urban transformation.

The Invisible Hand at Work

What ties together these diverse aspects of parking lot economics is the concept of the "invisible hand"—a term coined by economist Adam Smith to describe how individual actions, driven by self-interest, can collectively produce beneficial outcomes for society. Every time a driver chooses a parking spot, they are participating in a complex dance of economic forces. Their decision is influenced by price, convenience, personal preference, and even social signals, all of which are part of a larger, interconnected system.

The invisible hand in the parking lot is evident in how market forces self-regulate. If a particular area consistently experiences high demand and limited availability, prices will rise. This price increase, in turn, discourages some drivers from choosing that area, thereby balancing the demand. Conversely, if a lot is underutilized, lower prices may attract more drivers until equilibrium is reached. This self-regulatory mechanism, though simple in concept, mirrors the broader dynamics of free markets and serves as a microcosm of economic theory in action.

A New Perspective on Everyday Spaces

It is important to reflect on the broader implications of viewing parking lots as unseen marketplaces. What initially appears to be an unremarkable stretch of asphalt is, in fact, a living, breathing economic ecosystem. From the individual driver's split-second decision-making to the complex interplay of supply and demand, every facet of a parking lot is imbued with economic significance.

By reimagining parking lots as vibrant marketplaces, we open the door to a new perspective on the ordinary. In every decision to park a car, there is an interplay of economics, culture, and behavior—a microcosm of the invisible forces that drive our world. The unseen marketplace of parking is a reminder that even the most mundane aspects of life can reveal profound truths about the way we live, work, and interact with our surroundings.

As you continue through this book, I invite you to look at the next time you park your car with fresh eyes. Recognize that each parking space is more than just a resting place for your vehicle—it is a node in an expansive network of economic activity, a reflection of societal values, and a silent yet powerful testament to the forces that shape our urban landscapes. In this light, the parking lot transforms from an afterthought into a critical piece of the urban puzzle, offering endless opportunities for discovery and understanding.

Measuring Value in Open Spaces

Now, we turn our attention to one of the most fundamental questions of any market: How is value determined? In the case of parking spaces, value is measured not only in monetary terms but also in social, psychological, and even environmental dimensions. There is a multifaceted process in valuing parking spaces, examining pricing strategies, the implications of scarcity, and the hidden costs and benefits that shape the parking ecosystem. In doing so, we reveal how parking lots serve as informal economic laboratories—real-world settings where experiments in pricing and consumer behavior play out every day.

The Monetary Value of a Parking Space

Scarcity and Supply-Demand Dynamics

At its most basic level, a parking space is a scarce resource. In many urban environments, the number of available spots cannot meet the demand generated by thousands of vehicles. Scarcity drives up value, as seen in many other markets. In bustling downtown areas or near popular venues, the premium placed on a convenient spot reflects both its limited supply and the high demand. Just as diamonds become valuable due to their rarity, so too do parking spots in prime locations command a higher price.

Economic theory tells us that when demand outstrips supply, prices will rise. This is evident in the way parking prices escalate during peak hours or major events. Conversely, in locations where parking is abundant—such as suburban shopping centers or newly developed commercial areas—prices tend to be lower. The dynamic interplay between supply and demand is a cornerstone of parking economics and serves as a microcosm for understanding broader market behaviors.

Pricing Strategies: From Fixed Rates to Dynamic Models

Parking operators use a range of pricing strategies to manage this delicate balance between supply and demand. Traditionally, many parking lots and garages have relied on fixed-rate pricing. This model offers simplicity: a set fee for a given period regardless of the time of day or demand fluctuations. While fixed pricing is straightforward and predictable, it often fails to capture the real-time value of a parking space.

In recent years, dynamic pricing has emerged as a more sophisticated strategy. Borrowed from the airline and ride-sharing industries, dynamic pricing adjusts the cost of parking based on various factors such as time of day, occupancy rates, local events, and even weather conditions. For example, during a major sporting event or concert, prices might surge dramatically to reflect the temporary spike in demand. Conversely, during off-peak hours, operators might lower rates to attract more customers and increase occupancy.

Dynamic pricing not only maximizes revenue for parking operators but also provides important signals to consumers. When prices rise, drivers may be incentivized to seek alternative transportation or to arrive at a different time, thus smoothing out demand. In this way, parking lots become living examples of market efficiency, where pricing serves as a tool to balance resource allocation in real time.

The Role of Technology in Pricing

Technology has revolutionized the way parking spaces are priced and managed. Mobile apps and sensor technology now allow for real-time monitoring of occupancy and traffic patterns. These tools enable operators to adjust prices on the fly and provide drivers with up-to-date information about available spaces. For instance, an app might notify a user that a nearby garage is nearly full and suggest an alternative location with lower prices.

Beyond dynamic pricing, technology facilitates reservation systems that allow drivers to pre-book parking spaces. These systems add another layer to the valuation process by introducing the concept of "time value"—the idea that not only the location but also the guarantee of a spot at a specific time has inherent worth. When a driver reserves a parking spot in advance, they are essentially paying for the certainty and convenience that the space will be available upon arrival.

Beyond Dollars: The Social Value of Parking

The Psychological Impact of Proximity and Convenience

While monetary value is important, parking spaces also carry significant social and psychological weight. The location of a parking spot relative to an entrance, elevator, or public transportation hub can influence a driver's experience and satisfaction. In many ways, the convenience of a parking space can be as valuable as the money saved by choosing a cheaper, more distant option.

Consider the phenomenon of "premium parking" in a crowded lot. A spot located near the entrance of a busy office building or shopping center is often perceived as a status symbol. Occupying such a spot can confer a sense of privilege and ease, reducing the stress of finding parking in a congested environment. The social value of proximity is deeply rooted in our desire for convenience and our cultural association of time with money.

The Hidden Costs: Time, Stress, and Opportunity

While the monetary cost of parking is straightforward, the invisible costs can be more significant. Time is perhaps the most critical yet underappreciated cost. Every minute spent circling a lot in search of an available space represents lost time—time that could have been spent working, relaxing, or engaging in other productive activities. This opportunity cost is rarely reflected in the sticker price of a parking spot, yet it plays a crucial role in how drivers make decisions.

Stress is another intangible cost associated with parking. The frustration of a long walk from a distant lot, the anxiety of parking in a poorly lit area, or the risk of damage in a cramped space can all contribute to a negative experience. These factors, though difficult to quantify, influence consumer behavior just as much as a dollar amount. In many cases, drivers are willing to pay a premium to avoid these hidden costs, a phenomenon that mirrors broader consumer behavior in other markets where convenience and quality of service are prioritized.

Social Signaling and Status

Parking spaces can also serve as markers of social status. In many urban settings, the type of parking available to an individual is often a reflection of their economic standing. Luxury car owners, for instance, might be more likely to opt for reserved or valet parking services, which not only offer convenience but also signal exclusivity. This social signaling is a subtle yet powerful aspect of parking economics. It reinforces social hierarchies and influences consumer behavior by creating a visual shorthand for wealth and status.

In addition, the design and maintenance of a parking lot can impact its social value. A well-maintained, secure, and aesthetically pleasing parking area can elevate the perceived value of the entire location. On the other hand, a neglected lot with poor lighting and safety concerns can detract from the overall experience, even if the monetary price is low. Thus, the social value of parking is a complex interplay of physical attributes, perceived convenience, and the cultural significance attached to these spaces.

The Invisible Costs and Benefits: Externalities of Parking

Opportunity Costs and Environmental Impact

Every economic transaction carries with it a range of externalities—costs or benefits that are not directly reflected in the market price. In the case of parking, one of the most significant externalities is the opportunity cost associated with land use. Urban land is a finite resource, and every parking lot occupies space that could potentially be used for other, perhaps more productive, purposes such as housing, parks, or commercial development. This opportunity cost is often invisible in the daily transaction of parking but has long-term implications for urban planning and economic development.

Environmental costs represent another critical externality. Large expanses of paved parking lots contribute to urban heat islands, increase stormwater runoff, and reduce green space. These environmental impacts can lead to higher municipal costs and lower quality of life for residents. Conversely, the development of green parking lots—spaces that incorporate vegetation, permeable surfaces, and energy-efficient lighting—can mitigate some of these environmental harms. The invisible benefits of such innovations include reduced energy consumption, improved air quality, and enhanced urban aesthetics. These benefits, while not immediately apparent in the parking fee, add to the overall value of a parking space by aligning it with broader societal goals such as sustainability and environmental stewardship.

The Cost of Congestion and Inefficiency

Another hidden cost in the parking ecosystem is congestion. Inefficient parking systems can lead to wasted time and increased traffic, as drivers circle around in search of a spot. This not only elevates stress levels but also contributes to higher emissions and reduced overall efficiency in urban mobility. In some cities, smart parking technologies are being implemented to alleviate congestion by guiding drivers directly to available spaces. By reducing the time and fuel wasted in searching for parking, these systems create a net benefit for both the individual and the community, even if the direct monetary cost remains unchanged.

Congestion also imposes indirect economic costs on businesses and communities. For instance, if a popular shopping center is plagued by inadequate parking, potential customers may be deterred from visiting, leading to lost sales and reduced economic activity. The ripple effects of these inefficiencies underscore the importance of considering both the visible and invisible costs when evaluating the true value of parking spaces.

The Benefit of Data and Behavioral Insights

One of the less obvious benefits of parking lots as economic laboratories is the wealth of data they generate. Every parking transaction, every sensor reading, and every app interaction provides valuable insights into consumer behavior. By analyzing this data, economists and urban planners can identify patterns, optimize pricing strategies, and improve the overall efficiency of parking systems.

For example, data collected from smart parking systems can reveal peak usage times, average parking durations, and even preferences for particular locations within a lot. These insights allow operators to adjust pricing dynamically, allocate resources more effectively, and even design parking lots that better meet the needs of drivers. In this way, the invisible benefits of data collection extend far beyond individual transactions, contributing to the development of smarter, more responsive urban infrastructures.

Parking Lots as Informal Economic Laboratories

Real-World Experiments in Pricing

Parking lots provide a unique setting for observing economic principles in action. Unlike controlled laboratory experiments, the parking ecosystem is a living, breathing environment where real consumers make decisions based on actual costs and benefits. This makes parking lots ideal venues for testing new pricing models, measuring consumer responses, and refining economic theories.

Dynamic pricing experiments, for example, have been deployed in several cities to study how drivers react to variable rates. In these experiments, prices are adjusted in real time based on factors such as occupancy and time of day. Researchers have observed that when prices are increased during peak periods, some drivers opt to change their arrival times or choose alternative transportation methods. This behavioral shift not only confirms traditional supply-and-demand theories but also provides deeper insights into how modern consumers balance cost against convenience.

Consumer Behavior and Decision-Making

The decision-making process involved in selecting a parking space encapsulates many of the complexities of human behavior. Drivers weigh multiple factors: the cost of the parking spot, the time it takes to reach their destination, the safety of the area, and even the social implications of their choice. This multifaceted decision-making process makes parking an excellent case study for behavioral economics.

One interesting aspect of consumer behavior in parking lots is the concept of "satisficing" versus "optimizing." Rather than seeking the absolute best deal—which might involve extensive research and waiting—many drivers opt for a "good enough" solution that balances cost, convenience, and risk. This behavior reflects a broader trend in consumer decision-making where time constraints and cognitive limitations lead individuals to make satisfactory rather than optimal choices. By studying these patterns in parking lots, economists can gain insights into how real people make economic decisions in everyday life.

Technological Innovations and Their Economic Impact

Technological innovations are not only reshaping pricing models but also transforming the way consumers interact with parking spaces. Automated parking systems, for instance, promise to reduce human error and increase the efficiency of space usage. These systems can park cars with precision, potentially increasing the number of vehicles that can be accommodated in a given area. While the upfront cost of such technology may be high, the long-term benefits—measured in increased capacity, reduced congestion, and lower labor costs—could justify the investment.

Moreover, the integration of mobile apps and sensor networks is turning parking lots into rich data sources. Real-time information on occupancy, wait times, and pricing allows operators to continually refine their models, making incremental improvements that benefit both the consumer and the urban environment. As this technology evolves, parking lots are likely to become even more efficient, further blurring the lines between traditional static pricing and dynamic, data-driven models.

The Broader Implications of Parking Valuation

Urban Planning and Land Use

The economic valuation of parking spaces has significant implications for urban planning. As cities grapple with issues such as congestion, pollution, and limited land availability, the way parking is managed can have far-reaching consequences. For example, excessive land dedicated to parking in urban centers can hinder the development of more productive uses, such as housing, green spaces, or commercial activities. By understanding the true value of parking—both monetarily and socially—city planners can make more informed decisions about zoning, land use, and infrastructure investments.

Innovative approaches, such as shared parking facilities or dynamic pricing models that reflect real-time demand, can help optimize land use and reduce the overall environmental footprint of parking. In doing so, these strategies not only improve the efficiency of urban transportation but also contribute to broader societal goals such as sustainability and improved quality of life.

Social Equity and Accessibility

The value placed on parking spaces is also intertwined with issues of social equity. In many cities, the availability and cost of parking can disproportionately affect lower-income residents who may have fewer transportation options. High parking fees in central areas can act as a barrier, forcing those with limited means to rely on less convenient or less safe alternatives. By examining parking valuation through the lens of social equity, policymakers can design strategies that ensure a more balanced distribution of resources. Initiatives such as subsidized parking rates, improved public transit options, and the development of multi-use spaces that serve both vehicles and pedestrians can help mitigate these disparities.

Cultural Shifts and the Future of Mobility

Finally, the evolving valuation of parking spaces reflects broader cultural shifts in how we view mobility and urban living. As environmental concerns and technological advancements reshape our transportation landscape, traditional notions of car ownership and parking are being challenged. The rise of ride-sharing services, autonomous vehicles, and alternative transportation modes suggests that the economic model of parking may need to adapt to new realities. In this context, understanding the value of parking spaces today can provide critical insights into how these trends will evolve in the future.

For example, as cities invest more in public transit and cycling infrastructure, the demand for traditional parking may decrease. Conversely, the integration of autonomous vehicle technology could lead to innovative parking models where cars park themselves, reducing the need for vast expanses of open space. These shifts not only affect the monetary valuation of parking but also alter the social and cultural dimensions that underpin its value.

Case Studies: Valuation in Practice

To illustrate the complexities of measuring value in parking, let us consider several case studies from different urban contexts.

Downtown Metropolises

In major cities like New York, Tokyo, and London, parking is at a premium. In these densely populated areas, a single parking space in a central location can command exorbitant prices. The scarcity of space, combined with the high opportunity cost of time, results in dynamic pricing models that reflect both the monetary and social value of proximity. Here, parking is not merely a commodity but a reflection of the city's pulsating economic and social life. Operators in these cities often rely on real-time data to adjust prices throughout the day, ensuring that the limited resource is allocated efficiently.

Shopping Centers and Entertainment Venues

Large shopping malls and entertainment complexes present another interesting scenario. During peak shopping seasons or when major events are scheduled, parking lots near these venues transform into temporary high-demand markets. Dynamic pricing and surge fees are common, and operators must balance the need to maximize revenue with the risk of alienating potential customers. In these environments, the invisible costs—such as the stress of finding a spot and the potential loss of time—are key drivers of consumer behavior. Studies have shown that many shoppers are willing to pay extra for a spot closer to the venue, highlighting the intertwined nature of monetary value and convenience.

Suburban and Residential Areas

In suburban settings, where parking is often less of a daily concern, the valuation process is different. Here, parking spaces might be integrated into residential complexes or community centers. The pricing strategies in these areas tend to be more stable, with a focus on long-term contracts rather than dynamic, real-time adjustments. However, even in these contexts, the social value of parking—such as safety, convenience, and community aesthetics—plays a significant role. In some neighborhoods, reserved parking spots are seen as a premium amenity, and residents may even trade or sell these spaces, mirroring real estate markets on a smaller scale.

Looking Ahead: The Evolving Landscape of Parking Valuation

As urban environments continue to evolve, so too will the models we use to measure the value of parking spaces. The integration of advanced technologies, coupled with shifting cultural attitudes toward car ownership and mobility, suggests that the economics of parking is a field in constant flux.

The Promise of Smart Cities

The concept of the "smart city" brings with it the promise of more efficient, data-driven urban management. In smart cities, parking lots become interconnected nodes in a larger network of transportation and urban infrastructure. Sensors, cameras, and mobile apps work in concert to provide real-time data on parking availability, occupancy rates, and consumer behavior. This data not only informs dynamic pricing models but also helps urban planners optimize land use, reduce congestion, and improve overall quality of life.

Redefining Value in a Post-Car Era

Looking further into the future, one must consider the possibility that the very notion of parking may change as society moves toward a post-car era. With the advent of autonomous vehicles, ride-sharing, and a growing emphasis on sustainable transportation, the demand for traditional parking spaces may diminish. In such a scenario, the value of parking might shift from being a marker of convenience and status to a resource that is repurposed for other urban needs. The transition from a car-centric society to one where alternative forms of mobility predominate will likely redefine what it means to "value" open spaces in urban settings.

Policy Innovations and Economic Experimentation

Policymakers will play a crucial role in shaping the future landscape of parking valuation. By implementing measures such as congestion pricing, incentivized shared parking, and environmentally conscious zoning laws, cities can encourage behaviors that align with broader social goals. These policy innovations, when combined with the natural market experiments occurring in parking lots, create a feedback loop that continually refines the balance between monetary value and social benefit.

Integrating Monetary and Social Metrics

The measurement of value in open spaces, particularly in the realm of parking, is a complex undertaking that requires a holistic view. It is not enough to simply assign a dollar figure to a parking space; one must also consider the social, psychological, and environmental dimensions that contribute to its overall worth. From the dynamic interplay of supply and demand to the invisible costs of time, stress, and congestion, every factor plays a role in shaping the economic landscape of parking.

As we have seen, parking spaces serve as informal economic laboratories—settings where real-world experiments in pricing and consumer behavior yield insights that extend far beyond the parking lot itself. These insights help us understand how individuals make decisions, how technology and innovation can optimize resource allocation, and how societal trends influence the value we assign to even the most mundane aspects of our urban lives.

In sum, measuring value in open spaces is an exercise in integrating both tangible and intangible metrics. It challenges us to look beyond traditional economic indicators and consider the broader impact of our choices on quality of life, environmental sustainability, and social equity. The parking lot, with all its complexities and hidden dimensions, becomes a mirror reflecting the intricate dance of economic forces and human behavior that shape our modern world.

By measuring value in open spaces, we begin to appreciate the delicate balance between cost, convenience, and community—a balance that is continually negotiated in the daily rituals of parking. Whether through dynamic pricing models that adjust to real-time demand, technological innovations that streamline the search for a spot, or policy initiatives that seek to align parking practices with broader societal goals, the evolution of parking valuation offers a microcosm of the challenges and opportunities facing modern urban environments.

In reflecting on these insights, we are reminded that even the most ordinary spaces can harbor extraordinary complexity. As cities grow and change, the humble parking lot stands as a testament to the power of economic theory in action—an open space where the invisible hand of the market meets the palpable needs of a dynamic, ever-evolving society.

Behavioral Economics on the Lot

Every day, thousands of drivers engage in rapid-fire decision-making processes when choosing a parking spot—a process that reflects deep-seated cognitive biases, trade-offs between risk and reward, and the constant weighing of time versus convenience. In these everyday decisions, we can observe a microcosm of human behavior that offers profound insights into decision-making processes in broader economic and social contexts.

The Psychology of Parking: Why We Choose What We Do

When you approach a parking lot, you are met with an array of choices. Some spots are close to the entrance, while others lie at the far end of the lot. There are spaces that seem easier to maneuver into, and others that appear riskier because of tight angles or heavy traffic flows. What drives a driver's choice among these options? Behavioral economics suggests that our decisions are rarely as rational as classical economic theory might imply. Instead, they are influenced by cognitive biases, emotional states, and a host of contextual factors.

Cognitive Biases and Heuristics

One key factor influencing parking decisions is the use of cognitive shortcuts, or heuristics. These mental shortcuts allow individuals to make quick decisions without having to weigh every possible factor in detail. For instance, many drivers employ the "availability heuristic" by choosing spots that are immediately visible or that have been occupied by vehicles in similar situations in the past. The ease of recalling a particular pattern of parking behavior can make one spot seem more attractive than another, even if a more optimal spot exists elsewhere in the lot.

Another common bias is "loss aversion." According to this principle, people are more sensitive to potential losses than to equivalent gains. In a parking scenario, a driver might choose a spot close to the entrance—not necessarily because it minimizes time, but because it reduces the perceived risk of losing precious minutes in a congested lot. The fear of wasting time circling the lot often outweighs the potential benefit of saving a few dollars by parking further away. This bias can lead to what might be considered "irrational" decisions, where the cost-benefit analysis is heavily skewed by the prospect of loss.

Satisficing Versus Optimizing

The concept of satisficing—a term coined by Herbert Simon—plays a significant role in parking decisions. Rather than meticulously evaluating every possible parking spot to find the absolute best option (optimizing), most drivers settle for a solution that meets a minimum threshold of acceptability (satisficing). In the hectic environment of a busy parking lot, the perfect spot is often sacrificed in favor of a "good enough" option. This behavior is a practical response to time constraints and the mental fatigue associated with making numerous small decisions in rapid succession.

The Influence of Social Norms

Social norms and expectations also affect how we park. The layout of a parking lot, the behavior of other drivers, and even the type of vehicle you drive can all contribute to your decision-making process. For example, when arriving at a crowded lot, drivers may subconsciously follow the lead of others, choosing spots that are already popular. This herd behavior is a common phenomenon in many economic decisions and reflects a basic human desire to conform to perceived norms, even in a seemingly private decision like parking.

In some cases, social signaling comes into play. Parking near the entrance or in a well-maintained area can serve as an indirect signal of status or prudence. Conversely, a driver might deliberately avoid a particular section of a lot if it is associated with higher risk, whether of theft, damage, or simply the hassle of maneuvering through tight spaces. This subtle interplay of social expectations can lead to clusters of similar behaviors, reinforcing the perceived value of certain areas within the lot over others.

Time, Convenience, and the Cost of Opportunity

Time is money—a maxim that resonates particularly well in the context of parking decisions. When choosing a parking spot, drivers are constantly making implicit calculations about the value of their time versus the cost of convenience.

The Time-Cost Trade-Off

Imagine you're late for an appointment, and you enter a nearly full parking lot. You have two options: circle around in hopes of finding a spot close to the entrance or settle for a spot further away and risk arriving late. The decision here hinges on the perceived opportunity cost of time. Behavioral economists have long noted that the value of time is subjective and can vary dramatically based on one's current priorities and emotional state.

Drivers often display what might be called "time discounting" behavior—a tendency to prefer immediate convenience over potentially better, but delayed, outcomes. This means that if a driver is in a hurry, the proximity of a parking spot becomes significantly more valuable than if they had ample time. Conversely, if time is abundant, a driver might opt to park further away to save money, even if it means a longer walk.

The Role of Convenience in Stress Reduction

Time is not the only factor; the overall convenience of a parking spot plays a vital role in decision-making. Convenience here includes not only proximity to the destination but also ease of entry and exit, the perceived safety of the area, and the likelihood of damage or other hassles. In high-stress situations—such as when driving in unfamiliar areas or during inclement weather—the convenience factor is amplified. A spot that minimizes walking distance or offers a clear, unobstructed path to the destination can alleviate stress and create a more positive overall experience, even if it comes at a higher cost.

Real-world observations show that drivers are often willing to pay a premium for spots that promise reduced hassle and lower stress. This willingness to incur additional costs reflects a broader trend in consumer behavior, where the intangible benefits of convenience and peace of mind are factored into economic decisions, even if they cannot be easily quantified in monetary terms.

Opportunity Costs: Beyond Just Money

The opportunity cost of parking extends beyond the immediate monetary fee. Every minute spent searching for an ideal parking spot represents a loss of time that could be spent more productively elsewhere—whether that's working, socializing, or simply enjoying leisure time. This lost time can be thought of as an implicit cost, one that drivers intuitively incorporate into their decision-making process.

Studies have shown that when drivers are aware of the opportunity cost of their time, they are more likely to opt for a higher-priced parking option that guarantees convenience and a reduced search time. In this sense, parking behavior becomes a real-world laboratory for observing how individuals value time—a critical component of modern economic theory.

Risk and Reward: Weighing the Pros and Cons

Every parking decision involves an evaluation of risk versus reward. Drivers constantly assess the potential benefits of a particular spot against the inherent risks it may pose.

Perceived Risks in Parking Choices

The risks associated with parking can be both tangible and intangible. Tangible risks include the possibility of vehicle damage, theft, or an accident in a congested lot. Intangible risks might involve the stress of navigating a complicated parking structure or the potential embarrassment of making a poor parking choice. These risks are weighed against the rewards of convenience and cost savings.

For instance, a driver may decide against a spot that is particularly close to the entrance if it appears too risky due to heavy traffic or poor lighting. Conversely, a spot that seems less secure might be avoided even if it offers the benefit of saving a few minutes. The balancing act between risk and reward is a critical component of behavioral economics on the lot.

The Role of Uncertainty

Uncertainty is an inherent part of parking decisions. When you enter a new parking lot or even return to a familiar one under different circumstances (such as during a busy event), you face unknowns about availability, safety, and overall convenience. Behavioral economics tells us that uncertainty can lead to risk-averse behavior, where individuals prefer options that are perceived as "safer" even if they might be more expensive or less convenient.

This behavior can be observed in the way drivers often choose spots with clear lines of sight and easy exits, even if these spots are not optimally located in terms of walking distance. The reassurance of predictability and lower perceived risk often trumps the allure of a marginally closer spot that comes with heightened uncertainty.

Reward Sensitivity and the Allure of the "Perfect" Spot

On the flip side, the reward of finding the "perfect" parking spot—one that offers maximum convenience with minimal risk—is a powerful motivator. This reward is not solely financial; it is also psychological. The satisfaction derived from a well-executed parking maneuver or the relief of securing a coveted spot can trigger a positive emotional response. This response reinforces the behavior and can even lead to a form of behavioral conditioning, where drivers develop habits or preferences for certain areas of a parking lot.

In some experiments, drivers have been observed to circle multiple times before settling on a spot, seemingly in search of an ideal balance between risk and reward. While this behavior may appear inefficient, it underscores the complex psychological calculus at play. The drive to optimize personal comfort and minimize potential downsides leads to a dynamic interplay between decision-making and emotional satisfaction.

Real-World Observations and Experiments on the Lot

To better understand the behavioral economics behind parking, researchers have conducted numerous real-world experiments and observational studies. These studies not only validate theoretical models but also provide concrete examples of how drivers behave under varying conditions.

Experiment 1: The Dynamic Pricing Test

In one well-known study, researchers implemented a dynamic pricing model in a busy urban parking lot. The experiment varied parking fees based on real-time occupancy and peak traffic times. The findings revealed that as prices increased during peak hours, a significant number of drivers altered their behavior. Some chose to arrive earlier or later, effectively smoothing out the demand curve. Others opted for alternative transportation modes altogether, such as ride-sharing or public transit.

This experiment underscored the role of time and cost in decision-making. It also illustrated the elasticity of demand in response to pricing signals—a fundamental concept in behavioral economics. The dynamic pricing test demonstrated that drivers are not only responsive to the price of parking but also to the implicit cost of time and the psychological discomfort of uncertainty in a crowded lot.

Experiment 2: The Proximity versus Safety Dilemma

Another study focused on the trade-off between proximity to the destination and perceived safety. In a controlled setting, researchers varied the conditions of parking spaces within a lot—some spots were located near busy exits with heavy traffic, while others were in quieter, more isolated areas. Participants were asked to rate their comfort levels, perceived safety, and overall satisfaction with their chosen spot.

The results were illuminating. Many drivers reported a willingness to sacrifice proximity in exchange for a greater sense of safety and reduced stress. Even when a closer spot was available, the fear of potential hazards, such as other vehicles or poor lighting, led drivers to opt for the safer alternative. This experiment provided concrete evidence that behavioral factors—such as risk aversion and the desire for stress reduction—are powerful determinants in parking decisions.

Experiment 3: The Impact of Social Cues

Social cues also play a critical role in parking behavior. In one study, researchers observed drivers in different parking lots with varying social environments. In lots where other drivers were seen parking in orderly rows and leaving ample space between vehicles, newcomers were more likely to mimic this behavior. Conversely, in lots where vehicles were parked haphazardly and spaces were filled tightly, drivers tended to accept a more congested arrangement.

This phenomenon highlights the role of social conformity in decision-making. Even in an activity as seemingly mundane as parking, individuals look to their peers for guidance. The behavior of others acts as a heuristic, reducing the cognitive load associated with making complex decisions. These observations suggest that social norms, once established in a parking lot, can perpetuate certain behaviors, thereby influencing the overall dynamics of the space.

The Broader Implications for Human Decision-Making

The study of parking behavior is not merely an academic exercise; it has broader implications for our understanding of human decision-making in various contexts. The lot serves as a natural laboratory where principles of behavioral economics are played out in real time, offering lessons that can be applied to other areas of economic and social life.

Insights into Everyday Consumer Behavior

The patterns observed in parking decisions mirror those in many other consumer scenarios. For instance, the trade-offs between cost and convenience in parking are similar to those faced by consumers when choosing between different modes of transportation, grocery shopping options, or even online versus in-store purchasing. The same cognitive biases—loss aversion, satisficing, and risk aversion—appear in a wide range of settings. By studying parking behavior, economists gain insights that can help predict and influence consumer behavior in broader markets.

The Role of Emotions in Economic Decisions

One of the most striking insights from parking studies is the prominent role of emotions in economic decisions. Despite the rational underpinnings of classical economic models, real-world behavior often diverges from pure logic. Emotional factors such as stress, anxiety, and the satisfaction of achieving a "perfect" outcome heavily influence choices. This understanding has led to more nuanced economic models that incorporate psychological variables, offering a more complete picture of how people make decisions under pressure.

Policy Implications and Urban Planning

The findings from behavioral experiments on parking have significant implications for urban planning and public policy. For instance, understanding that drivers are willing to pay more for safety and reduced stress can inform the design of parking facilities. Cities might invest in improved lighting, clearer signage, or even dedicated "premium" zones that cater to drivers seeking convenience. Similarly, dynamic pricing models, refined through behavioral insights, can help manage congestion and reduce the environmental impact of circling for parking. These strategies demonstrate how insights from behavioral economics can lead to more efficient and humane urban environments.

Lessons for Risk Management

Risk and reward calculations are central not only to parking but also to many other aspects of life—from investment decisions to everyday consumer purchases. The observations made on parking lots regarding how people weigh potential risks against perceived rewards can be extrapolated to other areas where uncertainty and stress are factors. For instance, investors might exhibit similar patterns of risk aversion when markets are volatile, opting for safer, though less profitable, options. Understanding these parallels helps policymakers, business leaders, and financial advisors design systems and products that account for human behavioral tendencies rather than relying solely on rational models.

Strategies for Improving Parking Decisions

Given the insights gleaned from behavioral studies, it is possible to suggest strategies that could help drivers make better, less stressful parking decisions—while also improving the overall efficiency of parking lots.

Enhancing Information Transparency

One of the most effective ways to improve parking decisions is by enhancing the flow of information. Mobile apps and real-time signage can inform drivers of current occupancy levels, pricing fluctuations, and estimated walking times from various parts of the lot. When drivers have clear, accessible information, they are better equipped to weigh the trade-offs between cost, time, and risk. This transparency reduces the reliance on heuristics and allows for more informed, deliberate choices.

Designing for Behavioral Ease

Urban planners and parking lot designers can take cues from behavioral research to create environments that naturally guide drivers toward better decisions. This might involve designing lots with clearly marked "safe zones" that are well-lit and spacious, or organizing spaces in a way that minimizes conflict and congestion. When the environment is structured to reduce uncertainty and risk, drivers are less likely to experience decision fatigue, leading to smoother traffic flow and a more positive overall experience.

Incentivizing Optimal Choices

Incentives can be powerful tools in influencing behavior. Parking operators and city planners might consider offering discounts or rewards for drivers who choose less congested areas or who arrive during off-peak times. Such incentives not only help manage demand but also encourage drivers to adopt behaviors that contribute to overall efficiency. By aligning individual incentives with broader societal goals—such as reducing congestion and minimizing environmental impact—policy makers can harness behavioral insights to create win-win solutions.

Educational Campaigns and Behavioral Nudges

Finally, a combination of educational campaigns and subtle behavioral nudges can help shift driver habits over time. When drivers are made aware of the hidden costs of circling for a parking spot or the benefits of choosing a slightly less convenient option, they may be more likely to modify their behavior. For example, simple prompts on digital signage reminding drivers of the environmental impact of extra driving, or highlighting the time saved by selecting a certain area, can nudge individuals toward better choices.

Parking as a Window into Human Behavior

The humble parking lot, far from being a mere collection of concrete spaces, is a dynamic arena where human behavior, risk assessment, and the interplay of emotions and rationality come together in fascinating ways. Through our exploration of behavioral economics on the lot, we have seen how every parking decision is imbued with a host of psychological factors—from cognitive biases and heuristics to the intrinsic trade-offs between time, convenience, and risk.

These insights remind us that even in the most routine activities, such as parking a car, the principles of behavioral economics are at work. The patterns we observe on the lot are microcosms of larger economic and social behaviors that shape our everyday lives. Whether it is the instinct to minimize loss, the drive to secure a coveted position, or the influence of social norms, the choices made by drivers offer a valuable window into how humans navigate uncertainty and optimize their limited resources.

In studying parking behavior, we not only enhance our understanding of a specific urban challenge but also gain a richer appreciation for the complex interplay of factors that drive human decision-making. This understanding has the potential to inform improvements in urban planning, policy formulation, and even the design of consumer experiences in myriad other contexts.

As we close this chapter, the following key lessons emerge:

1. **Cognitive Biases Matter:** From loss aversion to satisficing, drivers rely on mental shortcuts that can lead to choices which may not be perfectly rational but are deeply rooted in human psychology.
2. **Time and Convenience Are Priceless:** The trade-off between time saved and money spent is a recurring theme in parking decisions, illustrating that the value of convenience often outweighs the nominal cost of a parking spot.
3. **Risk Influences Rewards:** Every parking decision involves an evaluation of potential risk versus anticipated reward. The balance of these factors determines whether a driver will opt for a spot that is closer, cheaper, or simply safer.
4. **Real-World Behavior Mirrors Broader Economic Patterns:** The observed behaviors in parking lots—such as dynamic responses to changing conditions and the impact of social cues—are reflective of broader consumer decision-making processes seen in various aspects of economic life.
5. **Data-Driven Strategies Enhance Efficiency:** By leveraging technology and behavioral insights,

> parking operators and urban planners can design systems that not only meet individual needs but also contribute to the overall efficiency and sustainability of urban environments.

Ultimately, parking lots serve as an everyday laboratory where the invisible forces of behavioral economics are made visible. They reveal that human decision-making is a complex tapestry woven from rational calculations, emotional responses, and social influences. As we continue to study these patterns, we move closer to understanding—and perhaps even predicting—the ways in which individuals respond to the myriad challenges of modern urban life.

The next time you find yourself circling a lot in search of that elusive perfect spot, remember that your decision is part of a grand experiment in human behavior. Each choice you make is a small, yet significant, example of the broader economic and psychological forces at work. In this light, the parking lot transforms from a mere utilitarian space into a powerful reflection of our collective decision-making processes—a reminder that even the simplest actions can provide profound insights into the human condition.

Cultural Codes and the Car Connection

When we think about parking lots, we often focus on their practical function—providing space for vehicles in busy urban and suburban landscapes. Yet, beyond the economics and behavioral dynamics lies a rich tapestry of cultural meaning. Parking spaces, and indeed the very act of parking, have evolved into symbols and rituals that reflect societal values about mobility, freedom, identity, and community. We will explore how parking lots serve as stages for cultural expression, uncovering the hidden codes that inform how we view cars, the spaces they occupy, and the broader implications of these associations in our daily lives.

The Car as a Cultural Artifact

Cars Beyond Transportation

Cars are far more than utilitarian machines for moving people from point A to point B; they are potent cultural artifacts. Throughout the 20th and 21st centuries, automobiles have come to symbolize personal freedom, modernity, and even rebellion. They are featured prominently in films, music, and literature as icons of individualism and status. The car one drives—and the way it is parked—communicates a wealth of information about personal tastes, social standing, and lifestyle choices. This symbolic value extends to the parking space itself, which becomes an extension of the car's identity.

For many, the car is an expression of self. Luxury vehicles, classic cars, and even customized rides become personal statements, and the choice of parking spot reinforces these messages. A pristine car parked in a well-lit, well-maintained lot not only signifies practicality but also the owner's commitment to status and self-image. In contrast, a weathered vehicle tucked away in a remote corner of a lot might reflect a different set of values—perhaps frugality, nostalgia, or even resistance to mainstream consumer culture.

Parking as a Performance of Identity

Every time a driver selects a parking spot, they are engaging in a subtle performance of identity. The act of parking is not a mindless mechanical process; it is laden with cultural significance. Consider the habitual practice of pulling into a reserved or "premium" spot near the entrance of a shopping center, office building, or restaurant. Such behavior communicates an unspoken message about the driver's priorities and social positioning. By choosing a spot that is more convenient or prestigious, drivers are participating in a social ritual that signals success, efficiency, or simply a desire to stand out.

This performance of identity is amplified by the design and context of the parking lot. In many urban centers, parking structures are designed with different levels or zones that subtly segregate spaces by convenience and perceived status. The "best" spots—those closest to the entrances, well-lit, and free of congestion—are often reserved (either explicitly or implicitly) for those who are deemed more worthy. In this way, parking spaces become a microcosm of larger social hierarchies.

Status Symbols and the Reserved Space

The Allure of the Prime Spot

In any busy parking lot, certain spots naturally acquire a reputation for being "premium." These coveted spaces are typically located near entrances, under canopies, or in areas that are well-patrolled and secure. For many drivers, securing one of these spots is about more than mere convenience; it is a subtle assertion of status. In a society that often equates success with proximity—whether that means being near the best seats at a show, the most desirable real estate, or the front of a line—the premium parking spot becomes a miniature version of this dynamic.

The importance of proximity is intertwined with notions of exclusivity. Just as front-row seats at a concert or a corner office in a skyscraper denote privilege, so too does a prime parking space. For corporate executives and high-net-worth individuals, a reserved parking space can serve as a tangible marker of success. Even in settings where parking is free or included with a service, the act of choosing or claiming a spot near the entrance carries an unspoken message about one's social position.

Reserved Parking and Social Segregation

The very practice of reserving parking spaces—whether through formal arrangements like designated spots for employees or through informal understandings among regular visitors—reflects broader cultural patterns of segregation and exclusivity. In many corporate and institutional settings, parking policies mirror hierarchies that exist in the organization. Senior management may enjoy reserved parking near the building's main entrance, while lower-level employees must park further away. This spatial arrangement is not accidental; it is a deliberate reinforcement of status and power within the organizational culture.

Similarly, in residential complexes and upscale neighborhoods, reserved parking spots are often marketed as exclusive amenities. They signal that the community is affluent and well-ordered, where every detail of daily life is carefully curated. Conversely, in areas where parking is less regulated or more chaotic, the absence of reserved spaces can reflect a different cultural ethos—one that values informality, egalitarianism, or even resistance to rigid social structures.

Parking Lots as Community Markers

The Shared Space and Its Social Dynamics

While individual parking decisions are often about personal identity and status, parking lots also function as communal spaces that reflect broader social dynamics. In many communities, parking lots serve as informal gathering places, where residents and visitors encounter one another and form a collective identity. This communal aspect is especially pronounced in suburban settings, where parking lots at shopping centers, community centers, and schools become extensions of the neighborhood itself.

In such environments, the design and management of parking spaces can influence the sense of community. For instance, well-lit and thoughtfully designed parking areas contribute to a feeling of safety and order, encouraging social interaction and fostering a sense of belonging. Conversely, poorly maintained or chaotic parking lots may signal neglect or discord within the community. The way parking spaces are organized—and the cultural codes that underpin these arrangements—therefore serves as a barometer for the health of the community at large.

Cultural Rituals and Shared Experiences

The ritualistic aspects of parking can also contribute to community identity. Consider the shared experience of arriving at a popular event or gathering, where drivers circle the lot together, exchanging nods or brief greetings as they search for an available spot. These moments of collective behavior, though fleeting, can create a sense of solidarity and shared purpose. In some cities, local traditions even emerge around parking practices—such as designated "meeting spots" in large lots where friends agree to convene, or particular areas that are known as the unofficial hubs of social activity.

This phenomenon is not confined to urban settings. In rural areas, the local parking lot might double as a venue for community events, farmers' markets, or impromptu social gatherings. Here, the parking space transcends its functional role and becomes a stage for cultural expression, where the everyday act of parking intersects with local traditions, social rituals, and even celebrations of community identity.

Cultural Expressions in Parking Design

Architecture and Aesthetics

The physical design of parking lots is itself a reflection of cultural values. In some cities, parking structures are designed to be visually striking, incorporating modern architectural elements that echo the broader aesthetic aspirations of the community. Sleek, glass-and-steel parking garages in metropolitan centers can be seen as monuments to technological progress and modernity, reinforcing the idea that even the mundane aspects of urban life are part of a larger cultural narrative.

On the other hand, some parking lots are designed with functionality and minimalism in mind, prioritizing efficiency over aesthetics. In these cases, the design reflects a different set of cultural priorities—those that value practicality, cost-effectiveness, and the utilitarian aspects of modern infrastructure. Yet even here, the layout, signage, and lighting all carry cultural codes that speak to local attitudes toward order, safety, and the role of public space.

Public Art and Community Expression

In many urban centers, parking structures have become canvases for public art and community expression. Murals, sculptures, and decorative lighting installations in or around parking lots transform these otherwise drab spaces into sites of cultural significance. Such artistic interventions not only beautify the area but also serve to communicate local narratives, histories, and values. They remind us that even spaces designed for the mundane act of parking can be repurposed as forums for cultural dialogue and creative expression.

In some cities, initiatives have been launched to integrate art into parking facilities as a means of reimagining urban landscapes. These projects often aim to challenge the perception of parking lots as lifeless expanses of concrete, instead highlighting their potential to serve as vibrant, multi-functional spaces that contribute to the cultural fabric of the community. The presence of art and design in parking areas underscores the idea that cultural expression is not limited to traditional venues like museums or theaters—it permeates every corner of urban life.

Mobility, Freedom, and the Car Connection

The Symbolism of the Open Road

At its core, the car is a symbol of mobility and freedom. The ability to travel independently, to explore new horizons on one's own terms, is a powerful cultural narrative that has been woven into the fabric of modern society. This narrative is particularly potent in cultures where the automobile represents not just a mode of transportation, but an extension of personal liberty and self-determination. In this light, parking becomes more than a logistical necessity—it is an integral part of the broader story of freedom that the car embodies.

The act of parking, then, can be seen as a momentary pause in the journey of freedom. It is a deliberate choice to claim a temporary space in a vast urban landscape—a place where the individual's connection to the car is on full display. Whether it's a sleek sports car parked proudly in a reserved spot or a vintage vehicle carefully tucked away in a corner, the parking decision reflects a complex interplay between the desire for mobility and the need for stability. The parking lot, in this sense, is a liminal space where the promise of the open road meets the realities of urban life.

The Car as an Extension of the Self

For many people, the car is almost an extension of their identity. It is a mobile home, a personal sanctuary, and often, a repository of memories. The way a car is maintained, the modifications it undergoes, and even the particular way it is parked can serve as indicators of the owner's personality and values. In many subcultures, the care and presentation of one's vehicle are taken very seriously, with enthusiasts investing significant time, money, and energy into customizing their cars. This commitment reinforces the cultural bond between the car and its owner—a bond that is further expressed in how and where the car is parked.

Parking then becomes a ritual that reaffirms this bond. A driver who takes great care in positioning their car just so, ensuring that it is perfectly aligned and presented, is engaging in a form of self-expression that goes beyond mere practicality. This meticulous approach to parking can be seen as a reflection of deeper cultural values such as attention to detail, pride in one's possessions, and a desire to be recognized within one's community. In this way, the parking lot becomes a stage on which personal narratives are played out—a place where cultural codes of respectability, competence, and individuality are continuously negotiated.

The Global Variations in Parking Culture

Regional Differences in Car Culture

The cultural significance of parking is not uniform across the globe. Different regions and cities imbue their parking practices with unique cultural codes that reflect local histories, urban planning philosophies, and social values. In many American cities, for example, the car is a central symbol of freedom and success, and parking lots are designed to accommodate this narrative with sprawling layouts, ample space, and emphasis on convenience. The open expanses of suburban parking lots, with their orderly rows and clearly marked spaces, reflect a cultural preference for order, individual space, and the idea of private ownership.

In contrast, many European cities, where urban density and historical infrastructure often limit parking space, have developed alternative cultural approaches. Here, the scarcity of parking is a well-known fact, and parking behavior is more a matter of pragmatism than status display. Yet even in these contexts, the act of finding a parking spot can be fraught with tension and imbued with cultural meaning. The ingenuity of parking solutions—such as mechanical parking garages and shared street parking—reflects a cultural commitment to efficiency, environmental sustainability, and the collective management of public space.

The Asian Perspective

Asian metropolises offer yet another perspective on parking culture. In cities like Tokyo and Singapore, where space is at a premium and urban planning is highly regulated, parking systems are often technologically advanced and meticulously organized. The emphasis here is on maximizing efficiency and minimizing congestion, and parking lots are designed to integrate seamlessly with public transportation systems. However, even in these contexts, parking remains a cultural marker. The precision with which vehicles are parked, the etiquette observed in crowded parking areas, and the design of parking facilities all reflect deeply ingrained cultural values such as discipline, order, and respect for shared space.

The Politics and Public Discourse of Parking

Parking as a Site of Civic Debate

The cultural codes surrounding parking are not confined to individual behavior or community aesthetics; they also extend into the realm of public policy and civic debate. In many cities, parking policy is a contentious issue, with debates centering on the allocation of public space, environmental impact, and social equity. The design and regulation of parking lots become proxies for broader political and cultural values. Should cities prioritize the convenience of car owners, or should they invest in public transit and pedestrian-friendly spaces? The answers to these questions are deeply rooted in cultural attitudes toward mobility, sustainability, and the role of government in regulating public life.

In debates over urban development, parking is often a flashpoint for discussions about the nature of progress and modernity. Proposals to reduce the number of parking spaces in city centers, for instance, are sometimes met with resistance from those who view cars as symbols of personal freedom and economic prosperity. Conversely, advocates for sustainable urban planning argue that reducing parking can lead to more livable, walkable cities—reflecting a cultural shift toward environmental consciousness and community well-being. These debates illustrate how parking, far from being a neutral or purely technical matter, is deeply enmeshed in the cultural and political fabric of society.

Media Representations and Cultural Narratives

Popular media plays a significant role in shaping our cultural understanding of parking and car culture. Movies, television shows, and literature often portray parking lots as microcosms of society—places where drama unfolds, identities are revealed, and societal norms are both reinforced and subverted. The portrayal of parking in film noir, for instance, with its dimly lit lots and tense, suspenseful moments, taps into cultural anxieties about urban anonymity and the dangers of modern life. In more lighthearted depictions, parking lots serve as backdrops for romantic comedies or as settings for humorous observations about modern convenience and the quirks of everyday behavior.

These cultural narratives not only reflect but also shape public attitudes toward cars and parking. They contribute to the mythos of the automobile as both a liberator and a potential source of conflict, a duality that is mirrored in the way parking spaces are valued and contested. Through these media representations, parking becomes imbued with layers of meaning that go far beyond its physical reality—a symbol of the tension between order and chaos, individual freedom and collective responsibility.

Reflections on the Cultural Codes of Parking

Parking as a Mirror of Societal Values

At its core, the act of parking reflects deep-seated cultural beliefs about how society should be organized and how individuals should relate to one another. Whether it is the emphasis on efficiency and order, the expression of individual identity, or the negotiation of social status, the parking lot encapsulates many of the cultural codes that underpin modern life. It is a place where the abstract ideals of freedom, mobility, and community are made tangible in the arrangement of concrete spaces and the behaviors of drivers.

Parking lots also force us to confront the contradictions inherent in modern society. The very idea of a parking space—a designated area for a private vehicle—stands in stark contrast to emerging trends in sustainability and shared mobility. As cities around the world grapple with issues of congestion, pollution, and urban sprawl, the cultural codes associated with parking are evolving. The shift toward alternative modes of transportation, the rise of ride-sharing, and the advent of autonomous vehicles all signal potential changes in how we value and interact with parking spaces. In this transitional moment, the cultural codes and the car connection are being renegotiated, offering a fascinating glimpse into the future of urban life.

The Future of Cultural Expression in Parking

As we move forward into an era of rapid technological and social change, the cultural significance of parking is likely to transform in unexpected ways. The traditional image of the car as the ultimate symbol of freedom may give way to new paradigms of mobility that emphasize shared experiences and environmental responsibility. In such a future, parking spaces might be repurposed entirely, transforming from static containers for vehicles into dynamic public spaces that serve multiple functions—community gathering areas, green spaces, or hubs for urban innovation.

Yet, even as these changes take hold, the cultural codes that have long governed our relationship with cars and parking are unlikely to vanish entirely. Instead, they will adapt, absorbing new meanings and contributing to an ever-evolving dialogue about identity, freedom, and community in the modern world. The ritual of parking, with all its subtle cues and cultural references, will continue to serve as a powerful reflection of who we are and what we value.

The Car Connection as a Cultural Lens

We have seen how the car, as a symbol of personal freedom and identity, carries with it a rich legacy of cultural meaning—one that is echoed in the choices we make about where to park. From the allure of the premium spot and the performance of identity to the communal dynamics and political debates that revolve around parking, every aspect of this everyday activity is charged with cultural significance.

Parking lots, in their quiet, unassuming way, serve as a microcosm of our cultural landscape. They mirror the societal values of efficiency, status, and community while simultaneously challenging us to rethink what it means to belong in an urban environment. The act of parking is not just a practical necessity—it is an expression of who we are, a ritual that encapsulates our desires for freedom, security, and recognition.

As our cities evolve and our modes of mobility change, the cultural codes associated with parking will undoubtedly continue to shift. Yet, the deep connection between cars and cultural identity will persist, serving as a reminder that even the most mundane aspects of modern life are imbued with meaning. By examining the cultural dimensions of parking, we gain not only a deeper understanding of urban life but also insights into the broader narratives that shape our collective experience.

In the end, the parking lot is more than an expanse of asphalt—it is a stage upon which the drama of modern life is played out. It is a place where economic, behavioral, and cultural forces converge, offering us a unique lens through which to view the complexities of contemporary society. As you step out of your car and into the world, take a moment to consider the cultural codes that surround you. In the simple act of parking, you are participating in a centuries-old dialogue about mobility, freedom, and identity—a dialogue that continues to evolve with every passing day.

The Social Geometry of Parking

When you step into a parking lot, you enter an environment that is far more complex than a random patchwork of asphalt and painted lines. Beneath the surface lies a carefully orchestrated spatial arrangement—a social geometry—that governs how drivers interact, how economic forces play out, and how subtle behavioral cues are communicated.

The Architecture of Interaction

Beyond Functionality: The Design of Social Spaces

At first glance, parking lots might seem to be nothing more than utilitarian structures designed to maximize the number of vehicles accommodated. Yet, much like urban plazas or office layouts, parking lots are imbued with a social purpose. The way spaces are delineated, the angles of parking spots, the positioning of barriers and walkways—all of these design elements contribute to an environment that dictates how drivers navigate, interact, and even feel.

Consider a parking lot designed with a generous central island and clearly defined lanes. This arrangement not only facilitates traffic flow but also creates a sense of order and predictability. Drivers are more likely to feel secure and less anxious when the environment signals clear direction and structure. In contrast, lots with confusing layouts, poorly marked boundaries, or obstructions can trigger stress, hesitation, and even aggressive behaviors as drivers try to negotiate ambiguity.

Spatial Arrangement as a Communication Tool

The spatial arrangement of parking spaces communicates much more than proximity to a destination. The design serves as a nonverbal language—a set of signals that guide social interaction. For instance, rows of neatly aligned spaces, uniformly spaced and equidistant from one another, send a message of equality and shared standards. On the other hand, irregular layouts, with some spots larger or more accessible than others, create an implicit hierarchy that influences behavior.

When drivers observe that certain spots are "better" than others—whether because they are closer to an entrance, under a canopy, or located in a well-lit area—they naturally infer that these spaces have higher social and economic value. In turn, these signals can shape behaviors such as competition for coveted spaces or even cooperative behaviors when drivers share information about available spots. The geometry of the parking lot thus becomes a powerful medium for social negotiation.

Hidden Signals in Layout and Design

The Language of Lines and Boundaries

Every painted line and marked boundary in a parking lot carries meaning. Lines that separate spaces are not merely practical guides; they also delineate personal territory. Just as physical boundaries in a home or office establish zones of privacy and ownership, so too do the lines in a parking lot signal where one driver's vehicle ends and another's begins.

These boundaries can reduce conflict when clear and well-maintained, but they can also become sources of tension if they are ambiguous. Faded lines or poorly defined spaces may lead drivers to contest territory, especially in high-demand lots. The precision and clarity of these markers can reduce aggressive behaviors by establishing unmistakable zones, while ambiguity can invite disputes over "extra" space or encroachment.

The Impact of Angles and Orientation

The angle at which cars are parked is another subtle yet significant element of social geometry. Perpendicular parking spots, angled parking, or even parallel parking each offer different advantages and disadvantages that extend beyond convenience. For instance, angled parking often allows for easier entry and exit, which can reduce frustration and the potential for minor collisions. However, it may also reduce the overall density of the lot, thereby signaling a commitment to driver comfort over maximum capacity.

Orientation plays a role in how drivers perceive their surroundings. A parking space that faces the lot's central area might encourage a more open interaction with other drivers, whereas spaces angled away from the main flow of traffic can foster a sense of isolation or territoriality. In other words, the design can either promote community and cooperation or fuel competition and defensive behavior, depending on the specific layout.

Signaling Safety and Security

Lighting, surveillance, and even landscaping within parking lots contribute to an overall sense of safety. A well-lit lot with clear sightlines not only deters crime but also reassures drivers, allowing them to navigate without fear. When drivers feel safe, they are more likely to exhibit cooperative behaviors—such as yielding to pedestrians or leaving space for others to maneuver. Conversely, poorly lit areas or spots that seem isolated can provoke defensive driving or even aggression.

The placement of security cameras and emergency call stations further reinforces the idea that these spaces are monitored and cared for. Such environmental cues play a vital role in calming the innate territorial instincts that might otherwise lead to conflict. In this sense, the social geometry of parking is closely intertwined with notions of public safety and communal trust.

Territoriality and Aggression on the Lot

The Psychology of Space Ownership

Humans have an intrinsic desire to claim and defend personal space. In the microcosm of a parking lot, this instinct is magnified. When a driver parks, they are effectively staking a claim—a small territory that they then feel compelled to protect. This territoriality is not necessarily aggressive in nature; rather, it is a natural extension of the need to secure one's property and personal safety.

However, when the available space is scarce, or when the boundaries between spaces are blurred, this instinct can quickly escalate into overt displays of aggression. A driver who perceives that another vehicle is encroaching on their "territory" may respond with honking, abrupt maneuvers, or even confrontational gestures. The layout of the parking lot can either mitigate or exacerbate these reactions. For example, lots that allow for ample space between vehicles tend to reduce the perception of crowding, thereby lowering the likelihood of aggressive behavior.

Aggression as a Function of Competition

In densely populated urban centers, the struggle for a desirable parking spot is a familiar sight. Aggression often emerges from the competitive nature of this search. Drivers may engage in risky maneuvers or display impatience when contending with others for a prime spot. The social geometry here is not just about physical layout; it is also a manifestation of the economic pressures and time constraints that many urban dwellers face.

Studies have shown that drivers in high-stress environments, such as busy downtown lots, are more likely to exhibit aggressive behaviors. These actions are often a direct response to the competitive context created by a limited supply of desirable parking spots. By contrast, in lots where space is more abundant or where the design allows for smoother traffic flow, aggression tends to be significantly lower. In this way, the spatial design of the parking environment directly influences the social behavior of its users.

Mitigating Conflict Through Design

Recognizing the potential for aggression and territorial disputes, urban planners and parking lot designers have experimented with various strategies to mitigate conflict. One approach is to incorporate "buffer zones"—areas between rows of parking spaces that provide additional room for maneuvering and reduce the likelihood of accidental encroachment. Such buffers not only enhance safety but also serve as visual cues that reinforce the idea of personal space.

Another strategy involves the use of visual markers that clearly delineate the boundaries of each parking space. High-contrast paint, reflective markers, and even physical barriers such as bollards can help ensure that each driver is aware of the limits of their territory. By reducing ambiguity, these design features lower the chances of disputes and create an environment where drivers can park with confidence and minimal stress.

Cooperation and Sharing in the Parking Ecosystem

Emergent Behaviors and Social Cooperation

While competition and territoriality are prominent features of parking behavior, they are not the only dynamics at play. Under the right conditions, parking lots can also be arenas for cooperation and shared social norms. Drivers often find themselves in situations where mutual courtesy and shared information can improve the overall experience for everyone.

For example, in a busy lot with ample space, drivers may slow down to allow others to merge or provide helpful signals when a spot opens up. These small acts of cooperation, though often unnoticed, contribute to a smoother flow of traffic and a more positive social atmosphere. The design of the parking lot can encourage these behaviors by reducing stress and uncertainty. A well-organized lot with clear directional signage and visible exits naturally promotes a sense of order, making cooperative behavior more likely.

Shared Spaces and Community Norms

Certain parking lots develop their own community norms over time. Regular users of a particular lot may establish informal rules about space usage, such as which rows are considered "safe" for quick exits or which areas are better suited for larger vehicles. These unwritten agreements can lead to a more harmonious environment where drivers share information and even assist one another when needed.

The social geometry of such lots reinforces these cooperative norms. For instance, lots with open layouts and communal gathering areas—such as a central island with seating or greenery—can serve as focal points for community interaction. In these settings, the parking lot transcends its original purpose as a vehicle repository and becomes a social space where people can meet, exchange ideas, and foster a sense of belonging.

Technological Aids to Cooperation

Modern technology is increasingly playing a role in fostering cooperation among drivers. Mobile applications that provide real-time information on available parking spots not only reduce the stress of circling a lot but also enable drivers to share valuable data with one another. In some cities, parking apps incorporate features that allow users to rate the safety and convenience of different areas within a lot, effectively crowdsourcing the social dynamics of the space.

These digital tools serve as an extension of the physical social geometry of the parking lot. By providing accurate, real-time data, they reduce uncertainty and help drivers make more informed choices. In turn, this technology encourages cooperation by reducing competition for scarce resources. When drivers are aware of alternative options and understand the layout of the lot, they are more likely to make choices that benefit not only themselves but also the collective user base.

Economic Outcomes Shaped by Spatial Dynamics

Pricing and the Value of Location

The geometry of a parking lot has significant economic implications. The location of a parking space—its proximity to an entrance, its visibility, or even its placement within the lot—can dramatically influence its perceived value. Premium spots, often located at the front or in areas with enhanced security and lighting, command higher prices and are more sought after by drivers. This spatial premium is a direct reflection of the underlying social geometry.

Dynamic pricing models in urban centers have begun to incorporate these spatial considerations. By analyzing the layout of a lot and the flow of traffic within it, operators can adjust pricing to reflect real-time demand. For instance, a spot that is consistently in high demand due to its favorable location might be priced higher during peak hours, while less desirable areas may be offered at a discount. This economic mechanism underscores the fact that spatial design is not merely an aesthetic concern but a fundamental component of market dynamics.

Efficiency and Resource Allocation

A well-designed parking lot maximizes the use of available space while minimizing the friction between individual drivers. Efficient spatial arrangements reduce the time spent searching for a spot and lower the overall stress associated with parking. From an economic perspective, this increased efficiency translates into lower opportunity costs and improved productivity for drivers. When a parking lot is designed to optimize flow and minimize conflict, it creates economic benefits that ripple throughout the urban environment.

The allocation of parking spaces also affects local businesses and urban planning strategies. In densely populated areas, the efficient design of parking lots can influence consumer behavior—encouraging shoppers to visit a retail center or prompting employees to choose a particular workplace. As cities grapple with issues of congestion and limited land use, the economic outcomes of parking lot design become an increasingly important factor in urban policy and planning.

Case Studies in Social Geometry

Urban Downtowns

In many bustling downtown areas, parking lots are more than mere parking facilities; they are integral parts of the urban landscape. In these settings, designers often incorporate features that not only address the functional needs of drivers but also foster social interaction. For example, some modern parking garages in metropolitan centers are designed with multiple levels of communal space, including green areas, seating, and even art installations. These features encourage drivers to view the parking facility as an extension of the public realm rather than a purely transactional space.

Such urban parking structures often feature clear signage, ample lighting, and designated zones that cater to different needs—whether it's a quick in-and-out space for shoppers or a secure, reserved area for office workers. The spatial layout in these cases not only boosts economic efficiency through dynamic pricing and optimized resource allocation but also enhances the overall social experience of parking. The resulting environment reduces aggression, promotes cooperation, and contributes to a more harmonious urban fabric.

Suburban and Community-Centric Models

Suburban parking lots, particularly those found in residential complexes or community centers, offer a contrasting but equally revealing example of social geometry in action. In these environments, parking is often closely tied to community identity. Lots are typically designed to promote safety and ease of access rather than maximum capacity. Features such as wide lanes, ample lighting, and clearly marked pedestrian pathways are common.

In these settings, the spatial design fosters cooperation among residents. Regular users of a community parking lot often develop informal social norms regarding space usage, yielding to neighbors, and even sharing information about available spots. The layout, with its emphasis on openness and clear boundaries, reduces the potential for conflict and creates a welcoming atmosphere where residents feel a sense of shared ownership. Such designs not only meet practical needs but also reinforce the communal values that define suburban life.

High-Density Innovations

Innovative parking models in high-density areas provide a glimpse into the future of social geometry. In cities where space is at a premium, new technologies and creative design solutions are transforming traditional parking lots. Automated parking systems, for example, rearrange vehicles in multi-level mechanical structures that maximize space efficiency while minimizing human error and territorial disputes. These systems rely on precise spatial algorithms that optimize the arrangement of vehicles, reducing the potential for conflict and ensuring smooth operation.

Moreover, some high-density parking facilities incorporate dynamic digital displays that guide drivers to available spots. These displays use data analytics to predict traffic flow and adjust the guidance in real time, further reducing the uncertainty that often leads to aggressive behavior. By seamlessly integrating technology with spatial design, these innovative models create an environment where both economic outcomes and social interactions are optimized.

Future Directions in Social Geometry and Parking Design

Integrating Smart Technology

The future of parking design lies in the integration of smart technology with an understanding of social geometry. As cities evolve into smart cities, parking lots will increasingly be outfitted with sensors, cameras, and data analytics systems that monitor usage patterns in real time. These systems can provide detailed insights into how drivers interact with the space, enabling operators to tweak layouts, adjust pricing, and implement measures that reduce conflict and enhance cooperation.

For instance, smart parking systems can identify areas of a lot that are prone to congestion or frequent territorial disputes. Operators can then redesign those areas—by adjusting the width of lanes, enhancing lighting, or introducing visual markers—to better manage traffic flow. Over time, these improvements can lead to a more harmonious balance between individual needs and communal efficiency.

Designing for a Changing Cultural Landscape

As societal attitudes toward mobility shift, so too will the design of parking facilities. The rise of alternative transportation modes, the advent of autonomous vehicles, and growing environmental consciousness will all influence how parking lots are structured. In a future where car ownership may decline in favor of shared mobility, the social geometry of parking may evolve from a focus on individual territoriality to one that emphasizes fluid, multipurpose spaces.

Imagine parking lots that transform after business hours into community hubs—areas where cars are parked in automated structures while the surface space is repurposed for events, markets, or green spaces. This repurposing would not only address urban congestion but also foster a sense of community by creating flexible spaces that encourage interaction and shared experiences. In such environments, the social geometry would be designed with adaptability in mind, ready to accommodate the evolving cultural narratives around mobility, sustainability, and urban living.

Policy and Urban Planning Implications

The insights gained from studying the social geometry of parking have significant implications for urban policy and planning. City planners who understand the subtle dynamics of space usage can craft policies that promote efficient, safe, and socially cohesive parking environments. For example, zoning regulations might be adjusted to encourage the inclusion of communal spaces in parking lots, or incentives could be offered to developers who incorporate smart, adaptive designs into their facilities.

Such policy innovations would not only improve the economic efficiency of parking but also enhance the overall quality of urban life. By aligning parking design with broader social and cultural goals, cities can create environments that are both functional and nurturing—spaces that reduce conflict, foster cooperation, and ultimately contribute to a more vibrant urban tapestry.

The Geometry of Our Shared Spaces

The social geometry of parking is a testament to the fact that even the most seemingly mundane environments are charged with layers of meaning and complexity. The spatial dynamics within a parking lot serve as a silent language—a language that communicates everything from the value of individual space to the unwritten rules of communal interaction. Through careful design and thoughtful management, parking lots can become arenas where aggression is minimized, cooperation is encouraged, and economic outcomes are optimized.

As we have seen, the layout and design of parking spaces affect how drivers interact with one another. Clear boundaries and well-defined zones reduce the potential for territorial disputes, while thoughtful orientation and lighting promote a sense of safety and community. These elements combine to create an environment that influences behavior on a fundamental level, demonstrating that the way we structure our built environments has profound social implications.

Moreover, the economic aspects of parking—such as dynamic pricing, resource allocation, and the value of location—are inextricably linked to these spatial dynamics. The "premium" spots in a lot are not just more convenient; they are imbued with social and cultural significance that reflects broader patterns of behavior and status. By understanding the social geometry of parking, we gain valuable insights into how space, design, and social interaction converge to shape both individual experiences and collective outcomes.

Looking ahead, the integration of smart technologies and adaptive design principles promises to transform parking lots into even more efficient, socially cohesive spaces. As cities continue to evolve, the lessons of social geometry will inform new models of urban infrastructure—models that prioritize safety, cooperation, and community engagement while addressing the practical challenges of modern mobility.

In the end, the parking lot is far more than a temporary holding area for vehicles. It is a microcosm of our social world—a carefully constructed environment where design, behavior, and economics intersect in fascinating ways. The hidden signals embedded in the geometry of these spaces remind us that our built environments are not passive backdrops but active participants in the dance of human interaction.

Every time you maneuver into a parking spot, you are engaging with a complex social system—a system that negotiates territoriality and cooperation, competition and community, individual rights and collective responsibilities. By appreciating the social geometry of parking, we come to understand that even the simplest act—finding a place to park—carries within it the echoes of larger social structures and cultural narratives.

As you leave your car in a lot, take a moment to observe the lines, the angles, and the subtle cues that guide your movements and those of others around you. In that observation, you will find a rich tapestry of social meaning—a geometry of human interaction that speaks to our shared need for order, safety, and connection. Ultimately, the parking lot, with its intricate design and social codes, stands as a silent yet powerful reminder that every space we inhabit is part of a larger dialogue about how we live together in an increasingly complex world.

Technology, Data, and the Future of Parking

In recent years, the parking landscape has experienced a dramatic transformation fueled by rapid advancements in technology. What was once a realm of concrete, painted lines, and manual transactions has evolved into a dynamic ecosystem of sensors, mobile applications, automation, and big data analytics. It also digs deep into the critical role that big data from parking systems plays in urban planning, economic forecasting, and the broader evolution of mobility.

In this new era, technology is not merely an add-on to existing parking infrastructure; it is the driving force behind a fundamental rethinking of how we allocate, use, and value parking. By integrating digital tools into every stage of the parking process—from finding a spot to paying for it—cities and private operators are creating systems that are more efficient, sustainable, and responsive to the needs of modern urban life. As we explore these developments, it becomes clear that the future of parking is inextricably linked to the growth of smart cities and the increasing reliance on data-driven decision-making.

The Rise of Real-Time Occupancy Sensors

How Occupancy Sensors Work

Real-time occupancy sensors are at the forefront of the technological revolution in parking. These devices, often embedded in parking structures or mounted above individual parking spaces, use a variety of detection methods—such as infrared, ultrasonic, or even video analytics—to monitor whether a parking spot is occupied. The data collected is transmitted to central management systems, which in turn provide drivers with up-to-the-minute information on space availability.

The sensors work by detecting the presence of a vehicle in a designated area and then relaying that information over wireless networks. This process happens continuously, ensuring that any changes in occupancy status are quickly updated. In many cases, these sensors are integrated with other smart city systems, creating a seamless flow of information that can be used to manage traffic, enforce parking regulations, or even adjust pricing in real time.

Enhancing Efficiency and Reducing Frustration

One of the primary benefits of real-time occupancy sensors is the dramatic improvement in parking efficiency. For drivers, the search for a parking spot can be a significant source of stress and wasted time. By providing accurate information about available spaces, sensors reduce the need for aimless driving and lower the risk of congestion. This technology not only enhances the driver experience but also contributes to reduced traffic emissions and better fuel efficiency by minimizing the time vehicles spend circulating in search of parking.

Integration with Navigation and Mobile Apps

Many cities and private operators have integrated real-time occupancy data with navigation systems and mobile apps.

Drivers can now receive notifications about available parking spaces before they even arrive in a parking lot, allowing them to plan their routes accordingly. These integrations enable dynamic rerouting and can even suggest alternative lots if the preferred location is full. By harnessing the power of GPS and real-time data, these systems create a seamless parking experience that transforms how urban mobility is managed.

Mobile Payment Systems: Convenience at Your Fingertips

The Evolution of Payment Methods

Mobile payment systems have revolutionized the transactional aspect of parking. In the past, drivers were often required to pay cash at a machine or interact with an attendant. Today, mobile apps and contactless payment technologies have replaced these outdated methods with seamless, digital transactions. These systems enable users to pay for parking using their smartphones, smartwatches, or even in-car interfaces.

The evolution from traditional payment methods to mobile platforms is driven by the need for speed, convenience, and integration with other digital services. Mobile payment systems offer features such as automatic billing, pre-paid reservations, and even time-extension options without the need to return to the vehicle. For busy urban dwellers, these innovations translate into significant time savings and a reduction in the frustration associated with parking fees.

Benefits for Operators and Cities

Mobile payment systems benefit not only drivers but also parking lot operators and city planners. For operators, digital payments provide faster transaction times, reduced labor costs, and lower incidences of fraud or human error. Cities benefit from improved revenue collection and enhanced data on parking usage patterns, which can be invaluable for urban planning and policy-making.

These systems also support dynamic pricing models, wherein parking fees are adjusted in real time based on demand. When integrated with occupancy sensors and other data sources, mobile payment platforms can automatically update prices and process transactions without any additional effort from the driver. This interconnected approach contributes to a more fluid and responsive parking ecosystem.

The Role of Contactless and Digital Wallet Technologies

With the rise of contactless payments and digital wallets, the act of paying for parking has become not only faster but also safer—especially in a post-pandemic world. These technologies reduce physical contact, thereby enhancing public health and safety. As digital wallets become more widespread, the future of parking transactions is likely to be entirely cashless, leading to further efficiencies in both operations and user experience.

Automated Parking Solutions: The Future of Vehicle Management

Understanding Automated Parking

Automated parking solutions represent one of the most futuristic aspects of parking technology. In these systems, vehicles are parked and retrieved by robotic mechanisms without any human intervention. Automated parking garages use mechanical systems to move cars to designated spaces, optimizing the use of available area while minimizing the need for large driving aisles.

The concept of automated parking is not entirely new; automated storage and retrieval systems have been used in warehouses for decades. However, applying these technologies to parking involves unique challenges such as vehicle safety, user interface design, and integration with existing transportation infrastructure. Recent advancements in robotics, sensor technology, and artificial intelligence have made automated parking a viable and increasingly attractive option for high-density urban areas.

Maximizing Space and Efficiency

One of the most compelling advantages of automated parking systems is their ability to maximize space efficiency. Traditional parking garages are designed to accommodate human drivers, requiring wide lanes and large turning radii. In contrast, automated systems can park vehicles in tighter configurations, effectively increasing the capacity of a given space. This is particularly valuable in densely populated urban centers where land is scarce and expensive.

Automated parking systems also reduce the risk of human error and accidents, as vehicles are moved by precision-guided machines. The increased efficiency not only benefits parking operators by maximizing revenue per square foot but also contributes to the overall reduction of urban congestion.

User Experience and Transition Challenges

Despite their many benefits, automated parking systems present unique challenges in terms of user acceptance and transition. For many drivers, the idea of relinquishing control over their vehicle to a machine can be disconcerting. To address these concerns, many operators are investing in user-friendly interfaces and transparent safety protocols that build trust and ensure a smooth transition.

Pilot projects around the world have shown promising results, with automated parking systems operating successfully in several high-profile urban developments. As these technologies mature and become more widespread, they are likely to reshape the very concept of parking, turning it from a time-consuming chore into an almost invisible part of the urban mobility experience.

Big Data: Unlocking Insights for Urban Planning and Economic Forecasting

The Data Deluge in Modern Parking

Every interaction within a modern parking system generates data. From occupancy sensor readings and mobile payment transactions to user behavior and dynamic pricing adjustments, vast amounts of information are being collected in real time. This data, when aggregated and analyzed, provides deep insights into patterns of mobility, consumer behavior, and urban infrastructure usage.

Big data in parking is more than just a tool for optimizing revenue—it is a rich resource for understanding urban dynamics. By analyzing parking data, city planners and economists can identify trends that might otherwise go unnoticed. For example, peak parking times, frequently occupied spots, and even the duration of parking can all provide clues about underlying economic activity and traffic patterns. Such insights are invaluable for making informed decisions about infrastructure investments, zoning changes, and public transportation initiatives.

Enhancing Urban Planning Through Data Analytics

Urban planners are increasingly turning to parking data to inform a wide range of policy decisions. Data analytics can reveal how different areas of a city are used, where bottlenecks occur, and how changes in infrastructure affect mobility. For instance, a sudden drop in parking occupancy in a particular neighborhood might indicate that residents are shifting to alternative transportation modes, such as biking or public transit. Conversely, an increase in parking demand could signal the growth of a commercial area or the need for additional transit options.

By integrating parking data with other sources—such as traffic sensors, public transportation usage, and even social media feeds—planners can develop a holistic view of urban mobility. This comprehensive understanding allows for more targeted interventions, ensuring that resources are allocated efficiently and that urban spaces evolve in ways that best serve their communities.

Economic Forecasting and Revenue Optimization

Beyond urban planning, big data from parking systems plays a crucial role in economic forecasting and revenue optimization. Operators can use data analytics to identify trends in parking demand, allowing them to adjust pricing models and improve revenue management. Dynamic pricing systems, which automatically adjust fees based on real-time demand, are powered by algorithms that continuously analyze parking data. These systems not only maximize revenue but also help balance supply and demand, reducing congestion and improving the overall efficiency of the parking ecosystem.

For city governments, accurate parking data can lead to more effective revenue forecasting and budgeting. By understanding the patterns of parking usage, municipalities can make better predictions about tax revenues, plan for future infrastructure needs, and design policies that encourage optimal use of urban space. In this way, big data becomes a critical component of the economic ecosystem, linking parking technology directly to broader fiscal and economic planning.

The Convergence of Technology and Sustainability

Reducing Environmental Impact

Technology-driven parking solutions have significant implications for sustainability. One of the major environmental challenges in urban areas is the excessive amount of fuel wasted as vehicles search for parking. Real-time occupancy sensors and navigation apps minimize this inefficiency, leading to fewer emissions and reduced traffic congestion. By streamlining the parking process, these technologies contribute to a greener, more sustainable urban environment.

Automated parking systems, by maximizing space efficiency, also help reduce the urban footprint of parking structures. With more vehicles accommodated in a smaller area, cities can reclaim valuable land for green spaces, pedestrian zones, or additional housing. The environmental benefits extend beyond reduced emissions—more efficient parking systems can contribute to improved air quality, reduced noise pollution, and even enhanced urban aesthetics.

Supporting the Transition to Electric and Autonomous Vehicles

As cities shift toward sustainable transportation, technology in parking is evolving to support electric and autonomous vehicles. Charging stations integrated into parking structures are becoming increasingly common, ensuring that electric vehicles can be parked and charged conveniently. Moreover, as autonomous vehicles begin to populate urban roads, the need for traditional parking is expected to change dramatically. Autonomous vehicles can drop passengers off and then park themselves in centralized hubs or even continue operating as part of a shared mobility service.

Data from parking systems is critical for planning these transitions. Understanding current parking usage, identifying potential locations for charging infrastructure, and forecasting future demand for autonomous vehicle parking are all essential components of a sustainable urban mobility strategy. In many ways, the evolution of parking technology is a microcosm of the broader transition toward a cleaner, more efficient transportation future.

Challenges and Opportunities in the Technological Revolution

Integration and Interoperability

While the potential of technology in parking is enormous, there are significant challenges to be addressed. One of the most pressing issues is the integration and interoperability of disparate systems. Many cities and private operators use a variety of technologies that do not always communicate seamlessly with one another. For instance, real-time occupancy sensors from one manufacturer might not easily integrate with a mobile payment system developed by another. Bridging these gaps requires standardization and collaboration across the industry.

Efforts are underway to create common platforms and protocols that allow different systems to share data and work together effectively. Such interoperability is essential not only for enhancing the user experience but also for harnessing the full power of big data analytics. As the technological ecosystem matures, we can expect to see increased emphasis on creating unified solutions that provide end-to-end integration from sensor to payment to data analysis.

Data Security and Privacy

With the collection of vast amounts of data comes the critical challenge of data security and privacy. Parking systems collect sensitive information about individuals' habits, locations, and financial transactions. Ensuring that this data is stored securely and used ethically is paramount. Breaches of parking data could lead to privacy violations or even be exploited for criminal purposes.

Operators and city governments must adopt robust cybersecurity measures and transparent data governance policies to protect users. As regulations around data privacy evolve, it will be essential for all stakeholders to remain vigilant and adapt to new standards. Balancing the benefits of data-driven innovation with the imperative of protecting individual privacy will be a defining challenge in the coming years.

Cost and Implementation Barriers

Implementing advanced technological solutions in parking infrastructure often involves significant upfront investment. For smaller municipalities or private operators with limited budgets, the cost of installing sensors, developing mobile apps, and integrating automated systems can be prohibitive. However, the long-term benefits—such as increased revenue, reduced congestion, and improved user satisfaction—often justify these investments.

Innovative financing models, public-private partnerships, and government grants are emerging as ways to overcome these cost barriers. As the technology becomes more widespread and mature, the costs are expected to decrease, making these advanced solutions accessible to a broader range of communities. In the meantime, early adopters can serve as models for how investment in technology can yield significant returns in terms of efficiency, sustainability, and economic growth.

Case Studies: Technology in Action

Urban Pioneers

Several major cities around the world have emerged as pioneers in the integration of technology into parking management. For example, Singapore has implemented an advanced parking system that combines real-time occupancy sensors with dynamic pricing and mobile payment solutions. The city's integrated approach has significantly reduced the time drivers spend searching for parking, leading to decreased traffic congestion and lower emissions. By leveraging data analytics, Singapore has also been able to optimize its urban planning efforts, adjusting infrastructure investments in response to actual parking usage patterns.

Private Sector Innovations

Private operators are also at the forefront of this technological revolution. Companies that manage large parking facilities in high-density urban centers have deployed automated parking systems that not only maximize capacity but also enhance the overall customer experience. In Europe, several commercial parking garages have been retrofitted with state-of-the-art sensor networks and mobile payment kiosks, transforming them into smart facilities that adjust pricing in real time based on occupancy and demand. These examples demonstrate that when technology is harnessed effectively, it can lead to both economic and social benefits.

Lessons from Pilot Programs

Pilot programs in various cities have provided valuable insights into the challenges and opportunities associated with new parking technologies. Trials of automated parking systems in select urban developments have shown that while initial user skepticism may be high, the long-term benefits—such as reduced search times, enhanced safety, and increased space efficiency—lead to broad acceptance over time. These pilots also highlight the importance of user education and support during the transition phase, ensuring that drivers understand how to interact with new systems and feel confident in their reliability.

Future Directions: The Next Frontier in Parking Technology

The Role of Artificial Intelligence and Machine Learning

Looking ahead, artificial intelligence (AI) and machine learning (ML) are poised to further transform the parking landscape. By analyzing vast amounts of data generated by sensors, payment systems, and user interactions, AI algorithms can predict parking demand, optimize resource allocation, and even forecast traffic patterns. These predictive models can inform everything from dynamic pricing strategies to long-term urban planning initiatives.

AI-driven systems could also enable more personalized parking experiences. For example, a smart parking app might learn a driver's preferences over time—such as the importance of proximity versus cost—and provide tailored recommendations that maximize both convenience and savings. As these technologies become more sophisticated, the line between parking management and urban mobility planning will continue to blur, paving the way for truly integrated smart city solutions.

Autonomous Vehicles and the Parking Revolution

One of the most significant shifts on the horizon is the advent of autonomous vehicles (AVs). As self-driving cars become a reality, the very concept of parking is likely to change. Autonomous vehicles could drop off passengers at designated hubs and then park themselves in remote, centralized facilities far from congested urban centers. This shift would free up prime urban real estate currently dedicated to parking and could lead to a radical reimagining of cityscapes.

In a future dominated by AVs, parking technology will need to evolve to support vehicle-to-infrastructure communication, remote management, and seamless integration with public transportation networks. The data generated by AV parking systems will provide even deeper insights into mobility patterns, enabling cities to adapt more rapidly to changing transportation dynamics. This convergence of autonomous technology and parking systems represents a frontier where technology, data, and urban planning intersect in exciting and transformative ways.

Collaborative and Open Data Platforms

To fully harness the potential of parking data, collaboration between public agencies, private operators, and technology providers will be essential. Open data platforms that allow for the sharing of anonymized parking information can accelerate innovation and improve decision-making across sectors. Such collaborative initiatives can help standardize data formats, ensure interoperability between systems, and enable a more comprehensive understanding of urban mobility patterns.

By fostering a collaborative ecosystem, cities can benefit from a wealth of insights that inform everything from traffic management to environmental policy. These open platforms may also encourage the development of third-party applications, further enhancing the parking experience for users and driving continuous innovation in the sector.

A New Era of Parking

The integration of technology and data into parking is not merely a technical upgrade—it represents a fundamental shift in how we conceptualize and manage urban space. Real-time occupancy sensors, mobile payment systems, automated parking solutions, and big data analytics are converging to create a parking ecosystem that is more efficient, sustainable, and responsive than ever before.

These innovations offer tangible benefits for drivers by reducing search times, lowering emissions, and streamlining the payment process. For operators and city planners, the wealth of data generated by these systems provides a powerful tool for optimizing resource allocation, forecasting demand, and making informed decisions that improve urban mobility and economic outcomes.

Looking to the future, emerging technologies such as artificial intelligence, machine learning, and autonomous vehicles promise to push the boundaries of what is possible in parking management. As cities continue to evolve into smart, connected ecosystems, the role of parking will expand from a mundane necessity into a vital component of urban strategy—one that reflects broader trends in sustainability, technology, and human behavior.

In this brave new world, parking is no longer an isolated, static element of urban infrastructure. It is a dynamic, data-rich environment that offers insights into the rhythms of city life and the economic forces that shape our communities. By embracing these technological innovations, we are not only enhancing the parking experience for individual drivers but also laying the groundwork for a more integrated, efficient, and sustainable future in urban mobility.

As you navigate your daily routine and use these technologies—whether through a smartphone app, an automated parking garage, or a real-time occupancy display—remember that you are participating in a larger transformation. Each interaction with a digital parking system is a small piece of a complex puzzle that is reshaping cities around the world. The future of parking is here, and it is powered by technology, driven by data, and destined to redefine how we experience urban life.

Policy, Regulation, and Public Space

In the intricate web of parking economics, public policy and urban planning serve as both the framework and the catalyst that shape how parking is allocated, priced, and experienced. Beyond the realms of market dynamics and consumer behavior, municipal regulations, zoning laws, and government initiatives have an outsized influence on the availability of parking spaces and the economic signals they transmit. We will scrutinize the intersection of parking economics with public policy, examining how zoning codes, municipal rules, and political decisions affect everything from the pricing of a single parking spot to broader patterns of social behavior in urban environments. By understanding these regulatory and policy frameworks, we gain insight into how public space is allocated and managed—and how such decisions ultimately affect the urban experience.

The Role of Zoning Laws in Shaping Parking

Zoning as a Tool for Urban Form

Zoning laws have long been used by cities as a means of organizing land use. They dictate the types of buildings that can be constructed in certain areas and outline the permissible uses of these spaces. In many cases, parking requirements are an integral part of zoning regulations. For example, a commercial zoning district might mandate that a new retail development provide a specific number of parking spaces per square foot of retail space, while a residential zone may require a certain number of spaces per dwelling unit. Such mandates are designed to ensure that sufficient parking is available to support anticipated demand, to reduce street congestion, and to promote accessibility.

These parking requirements have far-reaching effects. By dictating the amount of parking that must be provided, zoning laws indirectly shape the built environment. They influence the design of developments, the allocation of urban land, and even the aesthetics of public spaces. In areas with strict parking mandates, large parking lots or multi-story garages often become ubiquitous. This can lead to an urban landscape where parking dominates the visual and spatial character of neighborhoods—sometimes at the expense of pedestrian-friendly streets or green spaces.

Parking Minimums and Their Economic Impact

Mandatory parking minimums, which require developers to include a certain number of parking spaces in new projects, have been a standard policy in many cities for decades. While the intent behind these regulations is to reduce on-street parking demand and manage traffic flow, they often have unintended economic consequences. For one, parking minimums can increase the overall cost of a development. Developers are forced to allocate valuable real estate to parking—a use that may generate lower returns than other potential uses such as residential or commercial space. The additional cost is often passed on to consumers in the form of higher rents or property prices.

Moreover, parking minimums can distort market signals. When developers are compelled to build more parking than the market might naturally demand, it can lead to oversupply. An abundance of parking may depress the market value of individual parking spots, while simultaneously encouraging higher automobile use and further congestion. The result is a cycle in which excessive parking availability undermines alternative transportation modes, reinforces car dependency, and contributes to environmental degradation. In this context, parking minimums do more than just shape urban form—they send economic signals that can either encourage or discourage sustainable mobility practices.

The Debate Over Parking Maximums

In recent years, some cities have begun to challenge the traditional paradigm of parking minimums. An emerging trend is the adoption of parking maximums or the elimination of minimum requirements altogether. Advocates for parking maximums argue that reducing the amount of mandated parking can lead to more efficient land use, encourage public transit, and foster more walkable communities. By limiting the number of parking spaces that new developments must include, cities can reduce urban sprawl, lower construction costs, and free up space for other uses—such as parks, retail, or housing.

The debate over parking maximums reflects broader discussions about the future of urban mobility. Proponents of maximums believe that in an era of ride-sharing, autonomous vehicles, and improved public transit, the historical need for abundant parking is waning. They assert that excessive parking provisions can inadvertently encourage car use by making it too convenient and by subsidizing driving costs. On the other hand, critics argue that reducing parking requirements might lead to inadequate parking supply, particularly in areas where alternative transportation options are limited. The outcome of this debate has significant implications for urban planning, economic development, and social equity.

Municipal Regulations and the Pricing of Public Space

Dynamic Pricing and Government Intervention

Municipal regulations play a pivotal role in determining how parking is priced. Many cities have experimented with dynamic pricing models for on-street parking, in which rates fluctuate based on demand, time of day, and other variables. Such pricing strategies are designed to optimize the use of scarce urban space by balancing supply and demand. When implemented effectively, dynamic pricing can reduce congestion, encourage turnover, and ensure that parking remains available for those who truly need it.

The role of government intervention in parking pricing is complex. On one hand, cities have the authority to set parking rates through municipal policies, which can be used to manage demand and generate revenue. On the other hand, excessive regulation can stifle market responsiveness and lead to inefficiencies. For example, if parking rates are set too low by government mandate, they may fail to reflect the true cost of providing that space—including the opportunity cost of land

and the environmental impacts of car use. Conversely, if rates are too high, they may push drivers onto already congested streets or force them to seek alternative transportation methods.

The challenge for policymakers is to strike a balance between these competing priorities. By leveraging data and insights from smart parking technologies, cities can better calibrate dynamic pricing models to meet local needs. These models not only serve as tools for congestion management but also provide economic signals that guide drivers' behavior—encouraging them to consider alternative options when parking is at a premium. In doing so, dynamic pricing becomes a mechanism through which urban space is allocated more efficiently, reflecting both economic realities and public policy goals.

Public Parking Facilities: Ownership and Management

The management of public parking facilities represents another important intersection between policy and parking economics. In many cities, parking is provided by a mix of public and private entities. Municipal parking lots and garages are often operated by city agencies, while off-street parking in commercial developments is managed by private companies. The regulatory frameworks governing these different types of parking facilities can vary significantly, with implications for pricing, accessibility, and user experience.

Public parking facilities are typically viewed as extensions of the city's public space. As such, their management is often subject to greater public scrutiny and political oversight.

Governments must balance the need to generate revenue from these facilities with broader public policy objectives, such as reducing traffic congestion, promoting public transit, and ensuring equitable access to urban space. This balancing act is further complicated by the fact that parking revenue often forms a significant part of a city's budget, making any changes to pricing or allocation politically sensitive.

In many cases, cities are exploring innovative models for public parking management. For instance, some municipalities have partnered with private companies to operate public parking facilities under performance-based contracts. These public-private partnerships aim to combine the efficiency of the private sector with the public accountability of government, ultimately creating a more responsive and sustainable parking system. The success of these initiatives depends on the ability of policymakers to design contracts and regulations that align the interests of all stakeholders—ensuring that public space is managed in a way that benefits the community as a whole.

Impact on Social Behavior and Urban Livability

Parking regulations and pricing policies extend their influence beyond the realm of economics; they also shape social behavior and the quality of urban life. The availability and cost of parking affect where people choose to live, work, and socialize. For example, high parking fees in urban centers can discourage car use, prompting a shift toward public transit, biking, or walking. This, in turn, can lead to a more vibrant and pedestrian-friendly urban environment. Conversely, an overabundance of low-cost parking may incentivize car-dependent lifestyles, contributing to congestion, pollution, and a decline in the livability of urban spaces.

Municipal policies that promote efficient parking usage can have positive ripple effects on the social fabric of a city. By reducing the time and stress associated with finding a parking spot, well-designed parking systems improve the overall urban experience. They make it easier for people to access public spaces, local businesses, and community services—enhancing social interaction and fostering a sense of community. Moreover, when parking policies are aligned with broader sustainability goals, they contribute to environmental improvements that benefit public health and quality of life.

Cities that successfully integrate parking policy with urban planning often serve as models of livability and innovation. Initiatives such as "shared parking"—where multiple users access the same facility at different times—can optimize space usage while reducing the need for extensive parking infrastructure. Similarly, policies that encourage the conversion of underused parking lots into green spaces or community hubs are increasingly popular in forward-thinking cities. These approaches not only address the practical challenges of parking but also create public spaces that reflect the values of modern urban communities.

Government Initiatives and the Broader Urban Agenda

Transportation Demand Management and Parking

Government initiatives aimed at managing transportation demand have a direct bearing on parking policy. Transportation demand management (TDM) strategies are designed to reduce peak-hour traffic congestion, promote alternative transportation modes, and encourage more efficient use of infrastructure. Parking policy is a critical component of many TDM programs. By adjusting parking availability and pricing, cities can influence how and when people use their cars.

For example, some cities have implemented "congestion pricing" schemes that not only charge drivers for entering high-traffic zones but also adjust parking rates in those areas. Such measures create an economic incentive for drivers to consider alternatives to private car use. In turn, these policies help reduce congestion, lower emissions, and improve overall mobility. TDM strategies that integrate parking policy are part of a broader effort to create sustainable urban environments where mobility is balanced with quality of life.

Policy Innovations: Incentives, Rebates, and Beyond

In addition to pricing and zoning measures, governments have employed a range of policy innovations to shape parking behavior. Incentives such as rebates for using alternative transportation, tax breaks for developments that reduce parking requirements, and grants for the implementation of smart parking technologies are all examples of how policy can steer the market in desired directions. These initiatives recognize that parking is not an isolated issue but one that is deeply intertwined with urban economics, environmental sustainability, and social equity.

For instance, cities that offer incentives for carpooling or the use of electric vehicles indirectly reduce the pressure on parking infrastructure. Likewise, zoning policies that reward developers with reduced parking requirements in exchange for incorporating bike storage or public transit connections serve dual purposes: they encourage sustainable design while freeing up land for more valuable uses. Such policy innovations are vital for addressing the multifaceted challenges of urban parking in the 21st century.

Regulatory Frameworks for Emerging Technologies

The rapid evolution of parking technology has presented new challenges for regulators. As real-time occupancy sensors, mobile payment systems, and automated parking solutions become more prevalent, existing regulations often lag behind technological advancements. Policymakers are now tasked with updating regulatory frameworks to accommodate these innovations while ensuring fairness, safety, and accountability.

For example, regulations must address issues of data privacy and security in smart parking systems, ensuring that personal information is protected while still allowing cities to reap the benefits of data-driven decision-making. Similarly, as automated parking systems and autonomous vehicles begin to take hold, regulators need to consider new safety standards, liability issues, and integration protocols with existing transportation networks. These challenges require a proactive and forward-thinking approach, one that balances innovation with public interest.

The Interplay Between Public Policy and Economic Signals

Economic Implications of Parking Regulations

Parking policies send powerful economic signals that influence consumer behavior and shape urban markets. When governments impose parking minimums, for example, they are effectively subsidizing automobile use by ensuring that ample parking is available—often at the expense of other land uses. This can distort market signals and lead to inefficient allocation of urban space. Conversely, policies that reduce parking requirements can incentivize developers to build denser, more walkable communities, thereby shifting the urban fabric toward a more sustainable model.

Dynamic pricing policies, enforced through municipal regulation, also have significant economic implications. By tying parking fees to real-time demand, cities create a pricing mechanism that reflects the true cost of using urban space. This encourages drivers to consider alternative transportation options during peak periods and helps balance supply and demand. In this way, parking policy becomes a tool not only for managing congestion but also for signaling broader economic values—such as the cost of time, environmental impact, and the opportunity cost of land.

Social Behavior and Urban Equity

Parking policy does not just impact economic outcomes; it also shapes social behavior and urban equity. When parking is plentiful and inexpensive, it can encourage car-dependent lifestyles that marginalize alternative forms of transportation. This, in turn, can contribute to social inequities by favoring those who can afford private vehicles and disadvantaging those who rely on public transit. On the other hand, policies that limit parking availability or increase its cost can promote more equitable urban mobility—provided that robust public transit options are available as viable alternatives.

Cities that have successfully integrated parking policy with broader social goals often see improvements in both environmental sustainability and urban livability. For instance, reducing minimum parking requirements in favor of alternative transit investments can lead to more vibrant public spaces, lower congestion, and improved air quality. These benefits, while difficult to quantify in monetary terms, contribute significantly to the social fabric of urban communities. By aligning parking regulations with principles of social equity and sustainability, policymakers can foster environments that are not only economically efficient but also more inclusive and humane.

The Future of Public Space in an Evolving Urban Landscape

At its core, parking policy is a reflection of broader debates about the nature of public space in modern cities. As urban centers grow and evolve, the allocation of land for parking versus other uses—such as green spaces, residential development, or commercial activity—becomes a contentious issue. Many contemporary urban planners argue that excessive parking infrastructure is a relic of a bygone era of car dependency, one that must be reevaluated in light of new mobility trends and sustainability goals.

Government initiatives aimed at reclaiming public space often target parking structures as key areas for transformation. In some cities, underused parking lots are being repurposed into parks, community gardens, or cultural venues. These projects are not only a response to the changing demands of urban mobility but also a deliberate effort to redefine the role of public space. They reflect a broader cultural shift in which the value of urban land is measured not solely by its capacity to support automobile use but by its potential to enhance quality of life and foster community engagement.

Policy Case Studies and Global Perspectives

North American Approaches

Many North American cities have a long history of employing parking policies as a tool for urban management. In cities like Los Angeles and New York, parking minimums have traditionally been used to support sprawling suburban developments and ensure that car owners have access to convenient parking. However, in recent years, there has been a notable shift toward more progressive policies. Cities such as San Francisco and Toronto have started to relax parking requirements in downtown areas, incentivizing developments that prioritize walkability, cycling, and public transit. These changes are part of a broader trend toward reducing car dependency and promoting sustainable urban living.

European Innovations

European cities often provide a contrasting approach. In many European capitals, parking is treated as a scarce resource, and strict regulations are in place to limit the availability of on-street parking. Policies such as congestion charging and high parking fees in central districts serve to discourage private car use and promote public transit. In cities like London, Stockholm, and Amsterdam, urban planners have successfully integrated parking policy with wider transportation and environmental initiatives, resulting in cities that are both economically vibrant and environmentally sustainable.

Lessons from Asia

Asian megacities offer further insights into how parking policy can influence urban life. In cities such as Tokyo and Singapore, where space is at a premium, parking regulations are designed to maximize efficiency and minimize congestion. Singapore, for example, employs dynamic pricing and strict parking enforcement as part of its comprehensive transportation management strategy. The result is a highly efficient system where parking policy is seamlessly integrated with other aspects of urban planning, creating a model for cities around the world.

Challenges and Future Directions in Policy and Regulation

Balancing Stakeholder Interests

One of the greatest challenges facing policymakers is balancing the often-competing interests of various stakeholders. Developers, local businesses, residents, and environmental advocates all have a stake in how parking is regulated. Striking a balance that meets the needs of these diverse groups requires careful negotiation and evidence-based policy design. Transparent public consultation processes and data-driven decision-making are essential for crafting policies that are both effective and equitable.

Adapting to Rapid Technological Change

As parking technology continues to evolve—driven by innovations in sensors, mobile payments, and automated systems—regulatory frameworks must adapt accordingly. This calls for a flexible approach to policy that can accommodate new technologies without stifling innovation. Governments must work closely with industry stakeholders, urban planners, and technologists to ensure that regulatory reforms keep pace with technological advancements. Forward-thinking policies that anticipate future trends, rather than merely reacting to present conditions, will be key to ensuring a sustainable urban future.

Environmental and Social Sustainability

Looking ahead, the dual imperatives of environmental and social sustainability will increasingly shape parking policy. Cities are under mounting pressure to reduce greenhouse gas emissions, improve air quality, and create more livable urban environments. Parking regulations that promote reduced car dependency, efficient land use, and alternative transportation options will be crucial in achieving these goals. Moreover, policies that address social equity—ensuring that all residents have access to affordable, convenient mobility options—will be central to fostering inclusive, vibrant cities.

Crafting the Future of Urban Space

Public policy and regulation lie at the heart of parking economics, serving as the bridge between market dynamics and the lived experience of urban space. Zoning laws, municipal regulations, and government initiatives all play pivotal roles in shaping how parking is allocated, priced, and perceived. These policies have a profound impact not only on the economic signals embedded in the urban landscape but also on social behavior, environmental sustainability, and the quality of life in our cities.

By scrutinizing the intersection of parking economics with public policy, we uncover a complex tapestry in which every regulation, every zoning change, and every pricing decision is part of a larger dialogue about the future of urban space. The decisions made in city halls and planning commissions resonate on the streets—affecting where people live, work, and interact. They determine whether our cities become car-centric sprawls or vibrant, sustainable communities that prioritize people over vehicles.

As we move into an era marked by rapid technological change and growing environmental awareness, the need for innovative, forward-thinking parking policies has never been greater. The challenges are significant, but so are the opportunities. By aligning parking policy with broader urban goals—be they economic efficiency, social equity, or environmental sustainability—cities can create public spaces that enhance the urban experience for all residents.

Ultimately, the future of parking is not solely about managing cars; it is about crafting the very framework of urban life. As policymakers, urban planners, and community stakeholders collaborate to reimagine parking, they are also redefining what it means to inhabit and enjoy public space. In this process, parking regulations become more than just a means to an end—they transform into powerful instruments for shaping the cities of tomorrow.

In reflecting on the many layers of policy and regulation that govern parking, one is reminded that every decision has ripple effects. Whether it is a zoning amendment that reduces parking minimums, a dynamic pricing model that adjusts rates in real time, or a government initiative that repurposes underused lots into community spaces, these interventions send clear economic and social signals. They communicate values—about efficiency, sustainability, equity, and innovation—that ultimately define the character of our urban environments.

As you navigate your daily routines—whether you're searching for a parking spot in a busy downtown district or observing the carefully planned layouts of municipal garages—consider the broader forces at work. Behind each painted line and regulatory guideline lies a deliberate choice made by policymakers and planners, aimed at balancing the needs of a diverse urban population. In this light, parking is not simply a logistical necessity; it is a reflection of our collective vision for the future of public space.

As we look ahead, the integration of technology, data, and innovative policy will continue to transform parking into a dynamic tool for urban management. The insights gained from studying these intersections will guide future reforms, ensuring that parking policy evolves in step with the changing demands of our cities. In doing so, we have the opportunity not only to improve the efficiency of parking but also to enhance the quality of urban life, making our cities more sustainable, inclusive, and vibrant for generations to come.

Global Perspectives on Parking

When we consider parking, it is easy to imagine a uniform experience—a standardized grid of spaces in any given city. Yet, the reality is far more complex. Parking behavior and economics vary dramatically across the globe, influenced by cultural attitudes, urban design philosophies, economic imperatives, and even climatic conditions. We embark on a comparative analysis of how different regions manage parking spaces, how urban design shapes car culture worldwide, and what lessons can be gleaned from cities that have transformed parking from a mundane necessity into a dynamic economic asset.

Drawing on examples from North America, Europe, Asia, Latin America, and Africa, we will examine the multifaceted role parking plays in each context. We will explore the historical roots of parking policies, the modern innovations that are reshaping the landscape, and the broader social and economic implications of these approaches. In doing so, we will not only highlight the diversity of global parking practices but also underscore the universal challenges—such as congestion, sustainability, and land use—that cities everywhere must confront.

The Cultural and Economic Context of Parking Worldwide

Parking as a Reflection of Car Culture

In many parts of the world, the automobile is more than a mode of transportation—it is a cultural symbol. In North

America, for instance, the car has long been an emblem of personal freedom and suburban prosperity. Here, expansive parking lots and drive-through services underscore a lifestyle built around individual mobility and wide-open highways. In contrast, in densely populated European cities, where historic urban cores and narrow streets prevail, the car often assumes a secondary role. Instead, alternative transportation such as cycling, walking, and public transit are prioritized, and parking is a scarce commodity carefully regulated by municipal authorities.

Across Asia, the picture is equally varied. In cities like Tokyo and Singapore, where space is at a premium, parking policies are intricately tied to high-tech urban planning. Automated systems and dynamic pricing models are deployed to maximize the use of every square meter. Meanwhile, in emerging economies of Latin America and parts of Africa, rapid urbanization and growing car ownership have brought parking challenges into sharp focus, often revealing a tension between traditional urban forms and modern mobility demands.

Economic Forces and Urban Land Use

At the heart of global parking issues lies the fundamental economic question: How should limited urban land be allocated? In cities where real estate is exceptionally expensive, parking takes on a new dimension. For instance, in major metropolitan centers, a single parking space can be worth tens of thousands of dollars in opportunity cost. This has spurred innovative approaches to parking management that transform parking from a cost center into an economic asset. Some cities have even repurposed excess parking space into revenue-generating developments, parks, or cultural hubs.

Conversely, in sprawling suburban landscapes—common in North America—parking is abundant and often taken for granted. Here, the economics of parking tend to focus on convenience and efficiency rather than scarcity and premium pricing. The contrasting approaches illustrate how the interplay between land value, urban density, and mobility preferences drives diverse parking policies around the world.

North American Perspectives: Abundance, Suburban Sprawl, and Emerging Urban Challenges

The Suburban Paradigm

North America, and particularly the United States, has long been associated with the automobile. The post–World War II boom fostered a culture of suburban expansion, where single-family homes were built on vast plots of land with large driveways and expansive parking lots. In these environments, parking is plentiful. The design of shopping centers, office parks, and residential neighborhoods has traditionally prioritized ample parking to accommodate the car-centric lifestyle.

However, this abundance has come at a cost. The widespread availability of parking has often been cited as a subsidy for car ownership, contributing to traffic congestion, air pollution, and the sprawl that fragments communities. In recent years, urban centers like New York, Los Angeles, and Toronto have begun to reassess their parking policies in light of growing concerns over sustainability and urban livability. Efforts to reduce minimum parking requirements and promote alternative transportation have emerged as part of broader urban redevelopment strategies.

Dynamic Pricing and Smart Parking in the Urban Core

In response to urban congestion and environmental concerns, many North American cities are turning to technology to manage parking more efficiently. Dynamic pricing models, in which parking rates fluctuate based on real-time demand, are being tested on city streets and in municipal garages. These systems aim to reduce the frustration of cruising for a spot, lower emissions by decreasing the time vehicles spend searching for parking, and generate data that informs broader urban planning decisions.

The implementation of smart parking apps that guide drivers to available spaces represents another transformative trend. By integrating real-time occupancy data with navigation systems, these apps help urban dwellers avoid congested areas, thereby improving traffic flow and reducing the environmental footprint of parking. Such innovations illustrate a shift from a static, supply-driven approach to a dynamic, demand-responsive model of parking management in the urban core.

European Innovations: Scarcity, Sustainability, and the Shift Toward Alternative Mobility

Managing Scarcity in Historic Cities

European cities offer a striking contrast to the North American model, largely due to historical urban forms that predate the automobile. In cities like Paris, Rome, and London, narrow streets and centuries-old infrastructure mean that parking is both limited and highly regulated. Municipalities in these regions have developed sophisticated zoning laws and parking policies to manage this scarcity. High parking fees, restricted on-street parking zones, and rigorous enforcement are common tools used to discourage private car use in congested urban centers.

For example, London's Congestion Charge and the accompanying high parking rates in the city center are designed not only to manage traffic but also to promote alternative transportation modes. These policies reflect a broader commitment to sustainability and a recognition that the dense urban fabric cannot accommodate the same level of car dependency found in more sprawling cities.

Emphasis on Sustainability and Alternative Transit

European urban planning often prioritizes sustainability. Cities like Copenhagen and Amsterdam have famously invested in cycling infrastructure and public transit systems to reduce reliance on private vehicles. In these contexts, parking is not the primary focus; rather, it is managed as part of an integrated transportation strategy that values low-emission, multi-modal mobility.

Innovative solutions such as park-and-ride facilities are common in European cities. These facilities allow commuters to park their cars on the outskirts and complete their journeys via train, tram, or bicycle, thereby reducing inner-city congestion. Additionally, some cities have experimented with using dynamic pricing not only for on-street parking but also for off-street parking facilities. The resulting system encourages drivers to opt for less congested areas and supports a transition toward a more sustainable urban mobility model.

Transforming Parking into an Urban Asset

Europe's emphasis on reclaiming public space has led to innovative projects that repurpose parking facilities for broader community use. In cities where parking structures have become obsolete due to reduced car usage, these facilities are being converted into public parks, community centers, or mixed-use developments. For instance, in Paris, the transformation of parking garages into art galleries or green spaces has been part of a larger strategy to reimagine urban space and enhance the quality of city life. These initiatives not only address parking shortages but also signal a cultural shift away from car-centric planning toward a more people-oriented approach.

Asian Approaches: Technological Prowess and Space Efficiency

High-Density Urban Challenges

In many Asian megacities, such as Tokyo, Singapore, and Hong Kong, parking is a constant challenge due to extreme population densities and limited land availability. These cities have responded to the pressure by leveraging advanced technologies and innovative design solutions. In Tokyo, for example, automated parking systems and multi-level parking structures are common, maximizing the use of vertical space in an environment where every square meter is precious.

Singapore is another exemplar of technological ingenuity in parking management. The city-state has implemented dynamic pricing models, real-time occupancy sensors, and mobile payment systems to optimize the use of its scarce parking resources. In Singapore, parking is not just a necessity—it is managed as a strategic component of the city's overall transportation network. The integration of parking data with other urban systems allows for better traffic management, improved public transit planning, and a more efficient allocation of urban land.

The Role of Technology in Shaping Behavior

Asian cities are at the forefront of adopting technology to streamline parking and enhance user experience. Advanced sensor networks and surveillance systems provide granular data on parking usage, enabling authorities to implement dynamic pricing and enforce parking regulations with unprecedented precision. In addition, mobile apps in cities like Seoul offer real-time updates on parking availability, guide drivers to vacant spots, and even allow for cashless payments—all of which contribute to reduced congestion and smoother urban mobility.

The use of big data analytics in these contexts cannot be overstated. By harnessing data from myriad sensors and user interactions, city planners in Asia are able to forecast demand, adjust pricing in real time, and even reconfigure parking layouts to better match usage patterns. This data-driven approach not only improves operational efficiency but also informs long-term urban planning decisions, ensuring that parking infrastructure evolves in tandem with the rapidly changing urban landscape.

Cultural Nuances and Car Ownership

Cultural attitudes toward car ownership in Asia also shape parking policies. In many cities, owning a car is seen as a status symbol, yet the high cost of land and the efficiency of public transit systems mean that private vehicle ownership is less prevalent than in Western countries. As a result, parking facilities are often designed with flexibility in mind—they must accommodate both the occasional owner and the demands of a highly mobile urban population. In some cases, parking is integrated with other services, such as retail and dining, creating multi-use developments that serve as social hubs in addition to providing vehicle storage.

Latin American and African Perspectives: Rapid Urbanization and Adaptive Strategies

Latin American Urban Dynamics

Latin America presents a diverse array of parking challenges and solutions. In many rapidly growing cities like São Paulo, Mexico City, and Bogotá, urban sprawl and traffic congestion are pressing concerns. Here, the proliferation of cars has outpaced the development of adequate parking infrastructure, leading to a patchwork of formal and informal parking solutions. In some areas, street parking is the norm, with regulations that vary widely in enforcement and effectiveness. Meanwhile, private operators have stepped in to provide parking in key commercial districts, often at a premium.

Innovative projects in Latin America have focused on integrating parking policy with broader urban renewal initiatives. For example, some cities are experimenting with shared parking models that allow multiple users to access the same facility at different times of day. Such approaches not only maximize the use of limited urban space but also foster a sense of community by encouraging more efficient resource sharing. Additionally, efforts to digitize parking management—through mobile apps and real-time monitoring—are beginning to take hold, paving the way for more organized and efficient systems in the future.

African Urban Realities

In many African cities, rapid urbanization presents both challenges and opportunities for parking management. Metropolises like Lagos, Nairobi, and Johannesburg face enormous pressures as increasing numbers of residents and vehicles strain existing infrastructure. In these contexts, parking is often characterized by a mix of formal facilities and informal arrangements—street parking, open lots, and even makeshift parking areas coexist with more regulated parking garages.

Policy responses in African cities are increasingly geared toward modernizing parking infrastructure. Municipalities are exploring the use of technology—such as mobile payments and sensor networks—to better manage parking and reduce congestion. Furthermore, innovative urban planning initiatives aim to integrate parking with public transportation improvements, ensuring that the growth in vehicle numbers does not overwhelm city streets. Although resources can be limited, the adaptive strategies emerging in these cities offer valuable lessons in resilience and innovation.

Lessons in Flexibility and Resilience

Both Latin America and Africa illustrate the importance of flexibility in parking policy. In environments where formal infrastructure may be lacking or rapidly evolving, adaptive strategies—such as shared parking, public-private partnerships, and the integration of informal parking solutions—are critical. These regions demonstrate that effective parking management need not rely solely on high-tech solutions; sometimes, simple policy innovations and community-driven approaches can yield significant improvements in urban mobility and quality of life.

Transforming Parking into an Economic Asset

Reimagining Parking as Public Space

Across the globe, there is a growing recognition that parking facilities can be transformed into more than just repositories for vehicles. In many cities, underused parking lots are being reimagined as valuable public assets. The conversion of parking areas into parks, community centers, or mixed-use developments is gaining traction, particularly in cities that face challenges related to urban sprawl and declining quality of life. By repurposing parking space, municipalities can reclaim valuable land, foster social interaction, and stimulate economic activity.

Examples abound: In parts of Europe, abandoned parking garages have been converted into vibrant cultural venues or green spaces that invite community engagement. In some North American cities, parking structures are being redesigned as multi-functional hubs that include retail, residential, and office spaces. These transformations underscore a broader trend toward rethinking the urban landscape—one that recognizes the potential of parking not as a static, sunk cost, but as a dynamic, reconfigurable asset.

Dynamic Pricing and Economic Incentives

Innovative pricing models are also helping to reposition parking as an economic asset. Dynamic pricing, which adjusts parking fees based on real-time demand, has proven to be a powerful tool for managing congestion and optimizing resource allocation. By reflecting the true cost of parking—including the opportunity cost of land—dynamic pricing systems send clear economic signals to drivers. They encourage more efficient use of space, reduce the waste associated with excessive cruising, and generate valuable revenue that can be reinvested in urban infrastructure.

Cities that have successfully implemented dynamic pricing not only improve parking efficiency but also create a revenue stream that can support broader public projects. In many cases, the income generated from smart parking systems is earmarked for public transportation improvements, pedestrian-friendly initiatives, or environmental projects—thereby reinforcing the interconnectedness of parking policy and overall urban development.

Public-Private Partnerships and Innovation

Globally, public-private partnerships are emerging as a key strategy for transforming parking. These collaborations combine the efficiency and innovation of the private sector with the regulatory authority and public interest mandate of municipal governments. By working together, cities and private operators can develop parking solutions that are both economically viable and socially beneficial. Such partnerships often involve the adoption of advanced technologies, the creation of shared parking facilities, and the integration of parking with other urban services.

The success of these partnerships hinges on aligning incentives, sharing data transparently, and creating flexible regulatory frameworks that allow for experimentation. When done effectively, public-private collaborations can accelerate the adoption of innovative parking models, drive down costs, and enhance the overall urban experience.

Lessons Learned and Best Practices for Global Cities

Embracing Technology While Respecting Local Context

One of the key takeaways from a global perspective on parking is that technology, while transformative, must be adapted to local conditions. There is no one-size-fits-all solution. A system that works brilliantly in Tokyo may need significant modifications to function effectively in a sprawling American suburb or a historic European city center. Successful cities have struck a balance between high-tech solutions and local context, ensuring that innovations in parking management are both scalable and culturally appropriate.

Promoting Sustainability and Inclusivity

Another important lesson is the need to align parking policy with broader sustainability and social equity goals. Policies that prioritize reduced car dependency, promote alternative transit modes, and reclaim public space contribute not only to environmental sustainability but also to more equitable urban mobility. By integrating parking strategies with public transportation, urban planners can create more livable, inclusive cities that serve the needs of all residents—not just those who can afford a private vehicle.

Flexibility and Continuous Adaptation

Global parking practices also highlight the importance of flexibility in policymaking. Cities must remain agile, continuously collecting data and refining their strategies to respond to shifting mobility trends, technological advances, and changing social expectations. Adaptive policy frameworks, which incorporate real-time data and allow for iterative improvements, are essential for maintaining an effective parking system over the long term. This willingness to evolve is a hallmark of cities that successfully transform parking into an economic and social asset.

A Global Tapestry of Parking Practices

As we have seen, the world of parking is as diverse and dynamic as the cities in which it exists. From the sprawling, car-friendly suburbs of North America to the tightly regulated, sustainability-focused urban centers of Europe; from the technologically advanced, space-maximizing solutions of Asia to the adaptive, community-driven approaches emerging in Latin America and Africa—each region offers unique insights into the economics, culture, and urban planning of parking.

The global perspectives on parking underscore the fact that parking is far more than a logistical challenge; it is a reflection of our collective urban experience. It shapes and is shaped by cultural values, economic imperatives, and political decisions. Parking policies send powerful signals about what we value in our cities—efficiency, sustainability, accessibility, and community. They influence not only how we move, but also how we live, interact, and invest in our urban futures.

For policymakers, urban planners, and city dwellers alike, the lessons learned from global parking practices are clear. Innovation in parking—whether through technology, dynamic pricing, or public-private partnerships—can unlock significant economic benefits, reduce congestion, and enhance the overall quality of urban life. At the same time, the success of these innovations depends on their ability to respect local contexts, address environmental challenges, and promote social equity.

As cities continue to evolve in the face of rapid urbanization, technological change, and shifting cultural norms, the future of parking will undoubtedly play a central role in shaping the urban landscape. The transformative potential of parking—from converting underutilized spaces into vibrant public assets to using dynamic pricing to manage demand—offers a roadmap for creating smarter, more sustainable, and more inclusive cities around the world.

In reflecting on these global perspectives, it becomes evident that parking, often relegated to the background of urban planning discussions, is in fact a critical element of the urban tapestry. Every decision made about parking—from zoning laws and pricing strategies to technology investments and public-private partnerships—has far-reaching implications for the way we design our cities and live our lives.

Ultimately, by studying parking practices around the world, we gain valuable insights into the complex interplay between urban design, technology, culture, and economics. These insights not only help us address immediate parking challenges but also inform the broader quest to create cities that are resilient, efficient, and livable for future generations.

The Hidden Networks Beneath the Lot

At first glance, a parking lot might appear to be a simple collection of asphalt and painted lines—a static, utilitarian space dedicated solely to parking vehicles. Yet beneath this unassuming façade lies a complex, multilayered network of financial interests, real estate strategies, investment trends, and private negotiations that collectively shape the availability, pricing, and very existence of parking spaces. We pull back the curtain on the back-end economics of parking, revealing the hidden networks that govern this critical urban asset. We will examine how private interests, real estate markets, and investment trends converge to create intricate financial and strategic dimensions behind every parking spot. From the boardrooms of real estate developers to the spreadsheets of municipal finance departments, the story of parking is one of sophisticated economic interplay—a story that is rarely visible to the casual observer but is central to urban planning and economic strategy.

Beyond the Surface of Parking

Most drivers think of parking in terms of convenience, proximity, and cost. However, these decisions are influenced by a vast, behind-the-scenes network of stakeholders whose interests are deeply embedded in the fabric of urban development. While the consumer sees a fee paid at a meter or an app-based transaction, the real money is often made—or lost—by the entities managing parking assets. These networks determine how much parking is built, where it is located, how it is priced, and even how it is designed.

The back-end economics of parking involve a complex interplay between public policy and private profit. Municipal governments, private developers, real estate investors, and management companies are all key players. Their decisions, sometimes made in boardrooms far removed from the daily routines of drivers, ripple out to affect everything from the layout of a shopping center to the planning of a new high-rise. In exploring these hidden networks, we will see that parking is not just an afterthought in urban design; it is a highly valued asset with its own market dynamics and strategic importance.

Private Interests: The Corporate Side of Parking

The Rise of Private Parking Operators

In many cities, the management and operation of parking facilities have increasingly moved from the public sector to private hands. Private parking operators—ranging from local companies to multinational conglomerates—invest heavily in parking assets and employ sophisticated revenue management strategies. These operators view parking spaces as income-generating assets and work tirelessly to maximize their returns through dynamic pricing, real-time occupancy management, and targeted marketing.

Private operators often manage extensive portfolios that include surface lots, multi-level garages, and even on-street parking managed through digital platforms. Their business models rest on the ability to predict demand accurately, set optimal pricing, and ensure high turnover. For example, in urban centers where parking demand fluctuates dramatically with events, time of day, and even weather, private operators use advanced analytics to adjust prices in real time. This approach mirrors that of the airline or hotel industries, where supply and demand are in constant flux.

Corporate Strategies and Competitive Positioning

Behind every parking transaction is a web of corporate strategies aimed at capturing market share and ensuring profitability. Companies invest in technology not just for operational efficiency, but also as a competitive differentiator. By integrating mobile payment systems, real-time occupancy sensors, and data analytics platforms, private parking firms can offer a smoother user experience, reduce operational costs, and, ultimately, command higher fees.

The competitive landscape is intense. Firms compete for lucrative contracts with municipalities, shopping centers, airports, and corporate campuses. In many cases, securing a long-term contract for a large parking facility can provide stable, recurring revenue for decades—a particularly attractive proposition in a volatile economic environment. These contracts often include performance-based incentives, where the operator's revenue is tied to efficiency metrics such as turnover rates, occupancy levels, and customer satisfaction. In this way, private interests drive innovation and strategic investment in technologies that enhance the value of parking assets.

Lobbying and Policy Influence

Private parking operators are not just passive market participants; they are active lobbyists with significant influence over local and regional policies. In many cities, associations representing parking operators work closely with government officials to shape zoning laws, parking minimums, and even congestion pricing policies. Their lobbying efforts aim to create regulatory environments that favor private investment in parking infrastructure—often by establishing standards that guarantee a minimum return on investment or by reducing barriers to entry.

This influence can lead to policies that benefit the industry but may also have broader implications for urban development. For example, aggressive lobbying for higher parking minimums in new developments can lead to an oversupply of parking, which in turn encourages car dependency and urban sprawl. Conversely, a push for reduced parking requirements—often championed by transit advocates—can disrupt established revenue streams for private operators. The balance of these competing interests is a critical, yet often hidden, aspect of the parking economy.

Real Estate Markets and Parking as a Strategic Asset

Parking and Land Value: An Inseparable Relationship

At the heart of the back-end economics of parking is the intricate relationship between parking spaces and real estate markets. In densely populated urban centers, where land is scarce and expensive, the opportunity cost of parking becomes significant. A single parking space can represent a substantial portion of the land's value, particularly in areas where commercial and residential real estate prices are high. Developers and investors recognize that optimizing the use of parking can directly enhance the overall value of a property.

Consider a downtown high-rise office building: the availability of convenient parking can be a critical selling point, affecting not only tenant satisfaction but also the property's market value. In some cases, developers include underground or automated parking systems as part of the overall design strategy, positioning these facilities as premium amenities that justify higher rents. The hidden economic networks here involve complex negotiations over land use, property development rights, and the allocation of public subsidies—all of which are influenced by parking policy.

Investment Trends in Parking Facilities

Parking assets have increasingly become attractive investment vehicles for institutional investors, real estate investment trusts (REITs), and private equity firms. The relative stability of parking revenues—stemming from the essential nature of vehicle storage in urban areas—makes parking a compelling asset class in times of economic uncertainty. Investors are drawn to the predictable cash flows generated by parking fees and long-term contracts with municipalities and commercial operators.

The investment trends in parking are closely linked to broader shifts in urban development. In regions experiencing rapid urbanization, parking facilities can offer high yields due to the persistent demand for parking space. Conversely, in mature markets with slow growth, the focus may shift toward redeveloping or repurposing existing parking infrastructure to align with changing mobility patterns. This dynamic has led to a diverse array of investment strategies, ranging from the acquisition of large parking portfolios to the redevelopment of obsolete parking structures into mixed-use properties.

Real Estate Speculation and the "Parking Premium"

In many urban markets, the notion of a "parking premium" has emerged—a phenomenon where the value of a property is significantly enhanced by the availability of convenient parking. This premium is most pronounced in areas where on-street parking is scarce or where parking is heavily regulated. Developers, aware of the premium, may design projects that include an excess of parking spaces, even if market demand does not fully justify it, in order to maximize the property's appeal and resale value.

The financial strategies behind this phenomenon are complex. On one hand, providing ample parking can serve as a competitive advantage, attracting higher-paying tenants or buyers. On the other hand, overbuilding parking can lead to an oversupply that depresses prices. Investors and developers must therefore navigate a delicate balance between capturing the parking premium and avoiding the pitfalls of market saturation. The decisions made in this context are influenced by a range of factors—from local zoning laws and transportation trends to broader economic indicators and consumer behavior.

The Financial Engineering of Parking Assets

Structuring Deals and Revenue Streams

The financial engineering behind parking assets is a sophisticated field that involves structuring deals to maximize returns while managing risks. Parking assets are often packaged into investment vehicles that allow for diversification across multiple properties and geographic areas. This approach enables investors to hedge against local economic downturns or shifts in consumer behavior.

Revenue streams from parking assets can be highly variable, depending on factors such as location, usage patterns, and pricing strategies. To stabilize income, many deals incorporate long-term contracts with fixed or variable pricing formulas. These contracts often include clauses for performance incentives, escalation factors, and adjustments for inflation or changes in demand. The complexity of these financial instruments underscores the fact that parking is not simply a commodity sold on a per-hour basis; it is a financial asset that can be modeled, traded, and leveraged in ways similar to other forms of real estate.

Debt, Equity, and Risk Management

Like any significant real estate investment, parking projects are financed through a combination of debt and equity. Lenders and investors scrutinize the projected cash flows from parking fees, occupancy rates, and operating costs to determine the feasibility of a project. The relative predictability of parking revenue—often underpinned by municipal contracts or established market demand—can make parking projects an attractive proposition for conservative investors.

However, these investments are not without risk. Changes in urban mobility patterns, regulatory shifts, or economic downturns can disrupt expected cash flows. Financial engineers use sophisticated models to assess these risks, often employing stress tests, sensitivity analyses, and scenario planning. By modeling the potential impact of variables such as reduced demand, increased competition, or regulatory changes, investors can structure deals that mitigate risk and ensure stable returns over the long term.

The Role of Data and Analytics in Financial Decisions

In recent years, the availability of big data has transformed the way investors and operators manage parking assets. Detailed data on occupancy rates, user behavior, pricing fluctuations, and market trends enable a more granular analysis of parking performance. This data-driven approach allows for more accurate forecasting, improved operational efficiency, and better risk management.

For example, real-time data from occupancy sensors and mobile payment systems can feed into predictive models that forecast future demand and optimize pricing strategies. Investors use these insights to make informed decisions about acquisitions, renovations, or redevelopments. The integration of data analytics into financial decision-making has elevated parking from a static asset to a dynamic component of urban economics—one that responds to market signals in real time and offers actionable insights into the performance of urban infrastructure.

Strategic Dimensions: Beyond the Transaction

Parking as a Tool for Urban Influence

Beyond its role as a revenue generator, parking serves as a strategic asset that can be used to influence urban development. Control over parking assets often confers a degree of power in urban negotiations. For instance, cities may leverage parking concessions as part of broader agreements with developers, using the promise or restriction of parking facilities to shape the character of new developments. In this way, parking becomes a tool for urban influence—a means of steering investment, guiding urban design, and ultimately shaping the public realm.

The strategic use of parking extends to political influence as well. In many cities, parking revenue constitutes a significant portion of municipal budgets. Decisions about how parking fees are set, where parking facilities are located, and how revenue is reinvested can have profound implications for urban policy and governance. Stakeholders who control parking assets—whether private operators or public agencies—often wield considerable influence over urban planning decisions. This influence can be used to promote priorities such as economic development, sustainability, or social equity, depending on the strategic objectives of the decision-makers involved.

Negotiating Public-Private Partnerships

One of the most significant strategic trends in the back-end economics of parking is the rise of public-private partnerships (PPPs). These partnerships allow cities to leverage private sector expertise, capital, and technology while retaining a degree of public oversight and accountability. Through PPPs, municipalities can outsource the operation of parking facilities, share in the revenue generated, and even benefit from innovative technologies that improve service delivery.

The negotiation of these partnerships is a complex process that involves aligning the interests of multiple stakeholders. Public agencies must ensure that the terms of the agreement protect public interests—such as affordability, accessibility, and transparency—while private operators seek to maximize profitability and operational efficiency. The resulting contracts are often highly detailed, specifying everything from revenue-sharing arrangements and performance metrics to dispute resolution mechanisms. These agreements are a testament to the strategic importance of parking as an urban asset and highlight the hidden networks of power and finance that underpin everyday parking experiences.

Long-Term Urban Planning and the Future of Mobility

As urban mobility evolves with the advent of new technologies—such as autonomous vehicles, ride-sharing platforms, and electric mobility—the strategic dimensions of parking are also undergoing transformation. Forward-looking investors and planners are already considering how changes in transportation will impact the demand for parking, and they are reimagining parking assets accordingly. In some cases, parking structures are being designed with the flexibility to adapt to multiple uses over time. What begins as a parking facility might eventually be repurposed into community spaces, commercial hubs, or even residential developments.

This long-term perspective requires a deep understanding of market trends, technological innovation, and evolving consumer behavior. It also demands that stakeholders recognize the inherent value of parking assets beyond their immediate function. As cities strive to create more integrated, multimodal transportation networks, parking will continue to play a strategic role—not as an isolated commodity, but as part of a broader vision for sustainable urban development.

Hidden Networks and Their Broader Implications

The Invisible Hand of Financial Flows

The hidden networks beneath the lot are driven by flows of capital that often go unnoticed by the everyday user. The investments made in parking infrastructure, the financial instruments used to securitize parking revenue, and the complex negotiations that underpin public-private partnerships all contribute to a vibrant, if opaque, ecosystem. These financial flows are governed by market forces that, while invisible on the surface, have real consequences for urban form and public policy.

For example, when investors pour capital into parking facilities, they are often betting on the continued demand for parking in a car-dependent society. However, as urban mobility shifts, these financial bets may come under pressure. The transition to alternative transportation modes could alter demand dynamics, forcing investors to recalibrate their strategies. In this context, understanding the hidden networks of capital and finance is critical for anticipating how broader economic trends will impact the availability and cost of parking in the future.

Strategic Alliances and Competitive Dynamics

Within the hidden networks, strategic alliances are forged between developers, investors, technology providers, and government agencies. These alliances create competitive dynamics that shape the evolution of parking infrastructure. For instance, large real estate firms may partner with technology companies to develop smart parking solutions that give them a competitive edge in high-demand urban areas. Similarly, consortiums of investors may acquire portfolios of parking assets across multiple cities, allowing them to benefit from economies of scale and diversified revenue streams.

These alliances are not static; they evolve in response to market conditions, regulatory changes, and technological innovation. The competitive dynamics within these networks can drive rapid improvements in efficiency, as firms seek to outmaneuver each other through better pricing algorithms, superior technology integration, and more attractive financing models. The resulting innovations often have spillover effects on the broader urban economy, influencing everything from traffic patterns to urban land use.

The Social and Political Dimensions of Hidden Networks

It is important to recognize that the hidden networks beneath the lot are not solely financial in nature; they also have significant social and political dimensions. Decisions made by powerful investors or through lobbying efforts can have direct implications for social equity and urban quality of life. For example, aggressive expansion of parking facilities in suburban developments can contribute to car dependency, which in turn may marginalize residents who rely on public transit. Conversely, strategic investments in high-density urban parking—and the subsequent conversion of underutilized spaces into public amenities—can help create more livable, sustainable cities.

The influence of these networks often extends into the political realm, where parking revenue plays a role in municipal budgets and policy debates. The allocation of parking funds can influence everything from public transit subsidies to urban renewal projects. As such, the hidden networks of parking finance are also networks of power that shape urban governance and the distribution of public resources. Understanding these connections is essential for anyone interested in the future of urban development and the interplay between private profit and public good.

Unveiling the Layers of Urban Parking Economics

The hidden networks beneath the parking lot reveal a world where every parking space is far more than a simple commodity—it is the product of a vast, interconnected web of financial interests, real estate strategies, and investment trends. From private parking operators leveraging cutting-edge technology to maximize revenue, to real estate developers using parking as a strategic asset that can elevate property values, the back-end economics of parking are as complex as they are influential.

We have seen how private interests drive innovation and lobby for regulatory environments that favor profitable investments, while real estate markets imbue parking spaces with an economic premium that reflects land scarcity and urban density. Investment trends have transformed parking from a necessary afterthought into a key component of urban portfolios, with sophisticated financial models and risk management strategies underpinning every transaction.

Moreover, the strategic dimensions of parking—as tools for urban influence, instruments for public-private partnerships, and assets that shape long-term urban planning—demonstrate that parking is integral to the broader fabric of urban life. The hidden networks at work influence not only the financial performance of parking assets but also the way cities evolve, how public spaces are allocated, and how urban mobility is managed in a rapidly changing world.

As technology continues to advance and as global shifts in transportation alter the demand for parking, these hidden networks will undoubtedly adapt and transform. Investors, developers, and policymakers must remain agile, leveraging data and analytics to navigate a complex landscape where every parking spot is a strategic asset with both overt and subtle dimensions. The ability to understand and manage these hidden networks will be critical for crafting sustainable, resilient urban environments that balance private profit with public benefit.

Ultimately, the back-end economics of parking remind us that beneath every mundane transaction lies a rich tapestry of financial, strategic, and political considerations. The next time you pay for a parking space—whether at a municipal garage or a privately operated lot—remember that your payment is part of a much larger story. It is a story of private interests, real estate dynamics, and investment strategies that together shape the urban spaces we live in. By unveiling these hidden networks, we not only gain a deeper appreciation for the complexity of urban parking economics but also equip ourselves with the knowledge to influence the future of our cities for the better.

In the grand scheme of urban development, parking may seem trivial compared to skyscrapers, transit lines, or public parks. Yet it is precisely in these overlooked spaces that some of the most sophisticated economic and strategic battles are waged. The interplay of private interests, real estate speculation, and financial engineering drives decisions that affect every aspect of city life—from traffic congestion to urban aesthetics, from environmental sustainability to social equity.

As we continue to confront the challenges of urbanization in the 21st century, understanding these hidden networks will be essential. They not only reveal the economic underpinnings of parking but also serve as a microcosm of the broader forces at work in our urban landscapes. The lessons learned from the back-end economics of parking can inform public policy, inspire innovative business models, and ultimately contribute to the creation of cities that are both efficient and equitable.

Lessons Beyond the Asphalt

In many ways, a parking lot is an unlikely stage on which the drama of modern urban life unfolds. At first glance, it is nothing more than a patch of concrete and paint—a functional space designed solely to accommodate vehicles. However, as we have discovered, parking lots are microcosms of urban economics, culture, and human behavior. They embody the interplay of supply and demand, the influence of technology and public policy, the subtle language of spatial design, and even the hidden networks of finance that underpin urban development. In this concluding chapter, we extend the insights gleaned from parking lot economics to address broader societal and economic challenges. By understanding parking as an economic, cultural, and social phenomenon, we gain a new perspective on how we value and use space in our modern world—and we are called to rethink the assumptions that underlie urban life.

Parking as a Microcosm of Urban Dynamics

A Mirror for Economic Forces

Every time a driver searches for a parking space, they are engaging with a model of economic decision-making. The simple act of parking encapsulates the principles of supply and demand. In a high-demand urban center, scarce parking spots command premium prices, while an overabundance of spaces can depress value. This dynamic is not confined solely to parking—it is a reflection of how scarce resources are allocated in nearly every aspect of urban life. Whether it is real estate, labor, or time itself, the mechanisms of valuation are at play.

Parking lots, with their visible pricing strategies—from fixed rates to dynamic pricing models—offer an accessible way to understand market dynamics. They remind us that even everyday decisions are influenced by opportunity costs, externalities, and consumer behavior. When we see a driver hesitating between a premium spot near the entrance and a cheaper space farther away, we are witnessing, in miniature, the complex calculus that governs financial markets and business investments.

Lessons on Value and Efficiency

One of the most profound lessons from parking economics is that value is not intrinsic but is constructed through context and competition. A parking space in a bustling downtown district has a different value than one in a suburban shopping center. This principle applies to many aspects of urban life. The quality of a location—its proximity to amenities, its accessibility, its safety—directly influences its economic worth. By examining parking, we learn that our cities are, at their core, networks of interrelated value signals, where every square foot has a price determined by its connection to the broader fabric of the urban ecosystem.

Efficiency in resource allocation is another takeaway. Innovations in smart parking—real-time occupancy sensors, mobile payment systems, and automated parking solutions—demonstrate that technology can help reduce waste and improve outcomes. These systems minimize the time and fuel wasted as drivers circle in search of a spot, thereby lowering environmental impacts and reducing congestion. In broader terms, they suggest that integrating technology with urban planning can lead to more sustainable and efficient cities.

Cultural and Social Dimensions: Parking as a Reflection of Identity

The Cultural Codes of the Lot

Beyond its economic dimensions, parking is imbued with cultural significance. Our choice of parking spot often communicates messages about status, identity, and even social belonging. For many, the car is an extension of the self—a symbol of personal freedom and success—and the manner in which one parks reinforces these values. A neatly aligned car in a premium spot near the entrance can project an image of efficiency, care, and social standing. Conversely, a vehicle parked in a less desirable area may carry connotations of frugality or even rebellion against conventional norms.

In this light, the parking lot becomes a stage for cultural expression. The layout of the lot, the design of the spaces, and the unwritten rules of etiquette all contribute to a subtle but powerful social language. These cultural codes are not static; they evolve as cities change and as societal values shift. For instance, the growing emphasis on sustainability and alternative modes of transport is gradually altering traditional car-centric cultural norms, encouraging more equitable and environmentally friendly practices.

Social Behavior and Community Interaction

Parking behavior also sheds light on how individuals interact within public space. The territorial instincts displayed by drivers, the negotiation of shared space in crowded lots, and the unwritten rules that govern behavior all reflect broader patterns of human interaction. When drivers yield to one another, share information about available spots, or even develop informal norms about space usage, they are participating in a collective process that transcends the mere act of parking. These everyday interactions offer a window into how communities manage shared resources and how social order is maintained in seemingly chaotic urban settings.

Moreover, the social dynamics observed in parking lots have implications for urban design and policy. For example, when clear boundaries and well-designed spaces reduce conflict and foster cooperative behavior, they hint at the potential for creating more harmonious public spaces overall. Conversely, poorly planned parking can lead to stress, aggression, and even social fragmentation. The lessons learned here underscore the importance of thoughtful urban design that prioritizes both functionality and human experience.

Implications for Urban Planning and Public Policy

Rethinking the Use of Urban Space

One of the most compelling insights from parking economics is the realization that space is a finite, valuable resource that must be managed wisely. In many cities, parking lots and garages occupy vast tracts of land that could be repurposed for other uses—such as housing, parks, or community centers. The traditional emphasis on accommodating private vehicles is increasingly being questioned in light of growing environmental concerns, shifting mobility patterns, and the rise of alternative transportation modes.

The drive to repurpose parking spaces is not merely about reducing congestion; it is about reimagining urban life. By reclaiming underused parking areas and transforming them into multifunctional public spaces, cities can create environments that are more vibrant, sustainable, and equitable. This shift requires a fundamental rethinking of how we value space—not solely in monetary terms but also in terms of social and environmental benefits.

Policy Innovations for a Changing World

The lessons from parking economics also point to the need for innovative public policies that adapt to the evolving urban landscape. Municipalities around the world are experimenting with dynamic pricing, flexible zoning, and public-private partnerships to better manage parking and, by extension, urban mobility. Policies that adjust parking minimums, incentivize the use of public transit, or repurpose parking facilities for alternative uses are crucial in creating cities that are resilient in the face of rapid technological and societal change.

Dynamic pricing models, for instance, are not only a tool for managing congestion but also a mechanism for signaling the true cost of urban space. By reflecting the scarcity and desirability of parking, such models can help steer behavior in ways that align with broader urban goals—such as reducing traffic, lowering emissions, and promoting sustainable mobility.

Similarly, zoning reforms that allow for more flexible land use can enable cities to respond more dynamically to changing demand. When parking minimums are relaxed or eliminated, developers are free to allocate space in ways that better reflect the needs of modern urban residents—whether that means more green spaces, affordable housing, or mixed-use developments that encourage community interaction. These policy innovations demonstrate that by rethinking the role of parking, we can unlock broader benefits for society.

The Environmental Imperative

Parking economics also intersects with critical environmental challenges. The fuel wasted in searching for parking, the urban heat island effect caused by vast expanses of concrete, and the environmental cost of maintaining car-centric infrastructure all contribute to a growing awareness of the need for sustainable urban planning. Technology can help mitigate these issues—real-time occupancy sensors reduce cruising, while dynamic pricing discourages excessive car use. Yet the broader lesson is that our approach to parking must evolve in tandem with our environmental priorities.

Cities that prioritize environmental sustainability are increasingly looking to reduce the dependency on private vehicles by investing in public transit, cycling infrastructure, and pedestrian-friendly design. In this context, parking is re-envisioned not as a necessity for car travel, but as a resource that can be optimized or even repurposed to support a more sustainable urban ecosystem. The environmental imperative calls for a holistic approach that considers the full life cycle of urban infrastructure—from design and operation to repurposing and reinvention.

Insights into Human Behavior and Societal Values

The Subtle Signals of Everyday Choices

One of the most transformative lessons from studying parking lot economics is the realization that even the most mundane aspects of our daily routines are imbued with meaning. The decisions we make about where to park are not isolated transactions; they are reflective of our values, priorities, and even our identity. Every time a driver chooses a particular spot—whether out of convenience, status, or habit—they are participating in a broader economic and cultural dialogue. This dialogue extends far beyond the confines of the parking lot and speaks to the ways in which we structure our lives, allocate our time, and navigate the challenges of modern urban existence.

These subtle signals have broader implications. They remind us that human behavior is rarely purely rational; it is shaped by a complex interplay of cultural norms, social pressures, and individual preferences. By understanding these dynamics in the context of parking, we gain insights into larger patterns of decision-making and social organization. These insights can inform everything from marketing strategies to public policy, underscoring the value of a holistic approach to understanding human behavior.

Reassessing the Value of Space

Perhaps one of the most far-reaching lessons is the need to reassess how we value space in our modern world. In many traditional economic models, space is treated as a static commodity with a fixed value. However, the dynamic nature of parking—where the value of a space fluctuates based on demand, location, and time—challenges this notion. Urban space is not just a physical entity; it is a canvas upon which social, economic, and cultural values are projected.

By rethinking the value of space, we can begin to see opportunities for creating more vibrant, resilient, and equitable cities. For instance, the conversion of underused parking facilities into green spaces or community hubs is not simply an aesthetic or environmental improvement—it is a revaluation of urban space that prioritizes human well-being over vehicular convenience. This shift in perspective can lead to policies that encourage smarter, more sustainable use of land, ultimately enhancing the quality of life for urban residents.

Broader Implications for Economic and Social Policy

A Blueprint for Future Urban Development

The insights gleaned from parking lot economics offer a blueprint for addressing many of the challenges facing our cities today. The principles of dynamic pricing, efficient resource allocation, and technological integration can be applied to a wide range of urban systems, from public transportation to energy distribution. By viewing these systems through the lens of parking economics, we can identify strategies to optimize performance, reduce waste, and improve overall efficiency.

For instance, dynamic pricing models used in parking can serve as a model for congestion pricing in busy urban corridors. Real-time data collection and analytics, which have revolutionized parking management, can be leveraged to optimize traffic flow, reduce pollution, and improve public safety. These approaches highlight the potential for cross-sector innovation, where lessons learned in one area can be adapted to solve problems in another.

Redefining Public Space for the 21st Century

The transformation of parking spaces into multifunctional public assets is one of the most promising developments emerging from the study of parking economics. In many cities, vast tracts of land are currently devoted to parking—a relic of a bygone era of car dependency. By repurposing these areas for public use, cities can create new opportunities for social interaction, economic development, and environmental sustainability. Imagine a city where former parking lots become vibrant parks, cultural centers, or hubs for innovation—spaces that enhance the urban experience and contribute to a sense of community.

This redefinition of public space requires a fundamental shift in policy and planning. It calls for a move away from short-term, car-centric thinking toward a long-term vision that values flexibility, adaptability, and human-centered design. The lessons from parking economics remind us that urban space is not a static commodity; it is a living, evolving resource that must be managed with care and creativity. Policymakers, urban planners, and community stakeholders must work together to create cities that are not only efficient but also enriching and sustainable.

Social Equity and Inclusive Urban Mobility

Parking policy is intimately linked with issues of social equity and urban mobility. The availability and cost of parking can have profound impacts on who has access to urban opportunities and who is marginalized. In many cities, excessive parking subsidies have contributed to car-dependent lifestyles that disadvantage those who cannot afford private vehicles. Conversely, well-designed parking policies that encourage alternative transportation options can help create more inclusive urban environments.

By applying the lessons of parking economics to social policy, we can begin to address these disparities. For example, dynamic pricing and flexible zoning can be used to reduce the over-supply of parking in affluent areas, while investments in public transit and pedestrian infrastructure can ensure that all residents have access to affordable mobility. These measures are not merely about managing traffic—they are about creating cities that are fair, inclusive, and responsive to the needs of diverse communities.

Reflections on Human Behavior and Urban Culture

The Interconnectedness of Daily Decisions

As we step back and consider the broader implications of parking economics, it becomes clear that the simple act of parking is deeply interconnected with nearly every aspect of urban life. From the financial strategies of real estate developers to the cultural signals conveyed by our vehicle choices, parking reflects the complex tapestry of human behavior and societal values. Each decision—whether consciously made or driven by habit—contributes to the larger patterns that shape our cities.

The interplay between individual choices and collective outcomes is a recurring theme. Just as the decision to park in a premium spot affects traffic patterns and urban congestion, so too do our everyday choices influence larger economic and social trends. By understanding these connections, we can design systems that not only optimize individual convenience but also enhance the collective good. This holistic perspective is essential for addressing the multifaceted challenges of modern urban life.

Rethinking Values in a Changing World

One of the most profound lessons beyond the asphalt is the need to rethink how we value things. For too long, the focus on quantitative metrics—such as square footage or hourly rates—has overshadowed the qualitative aspects of urban living. Yet, as we have seen, the true value of space is multifaceted. It includes economic efficiency, social well-being, cultural expression, and environmental sustainability. This broader view of value challenges us to look beyond the immediate costs and benefits of parking, and to consider the long-term implications of how we design, manage, and inhabit our cities.

By adopting this more nuanced perspective, we can begin to prioritize investments that deliver lasting benefits. It is not enough to build more parking garages or expand roadways; we must also invest in the quality of our public spaces, the sustainability of our transportation systems, and the inclusivity of our urban communities. The lessons from parking economics thus serve as a call to action—a reminder that the choices we make about space have far-reaching consequences for our collective future.

Toward a New Urban Paradigm

Embracing Complexity and Interdisciplinarity

One of the key takeaways from our exploration of parking lot economics is that urban systems are inherently complex and interconnected. Solutions to urban challenges cannot be one-dimensional; they require an interdisciplinary approach that brings together insights from economics, sociology, urban planning, environmental science, and technology. The study of parking is a prime example of this integrative thinking. It shows that even the most seemingly mundane aspects of urban life are influenced by a myriad of factors and can offer profound lessons for broader societal challenges.

Embracing this complexity means acknowledging that every urban decision—no matter how small—has ripple effects. It requires a willingness to look beyond traditional silos and to foster collaboration among diverse stakeholders. Such an approach can lead to more innovative, resilient, and adaptive urban systems that are better equipped to meet the challenges of the 21st century.

Cultivating a Culture of Innovation and Adaptability

The rapidly changing nature of technology, mobility, and urban demographics calls for a culture of innovation and adaptability. Cities that have successfully integrated smart parking systems, dynamic pricing, and flexible zoning are not only managing today's challenges—they are also preparing for the future. These innovations are emblematic of a broader shift toward data-driven decision-making and responsive urban governance.

In cultivating such a culture, policymakers and urban planners must be open to experimentation and iterative learning. The lessons from parking economics encourage us to view urban spaces as living laboratories—places where new ideas can be tested, refined, and scaled up. By fostering an environment that embraces change and rewards creative solutions, we can build cities that are not only efficient but also vibrant and inclusive.

Reimagining the Urban Experience

Ultimately, the insights gained from parking lot economics invite us to reimagine the urban experience. They challenge us to look at our cities with fresh eyes—recognizing that every parking spot, every street, and every public space is a canvas on which the story of modern life is written. This reimagining is not merely academic; it has practical implications for how we design our neighborhoods, invest in infrastructure, and allocate public resources.

Imagine a city where underutilized parking lots are transformed into dynamic public spaces that foster community interaction and environmental sustainability. Picture urban centers where technology and policy work in harmony to reduce congestion, enhance mobility, and create a more equitable distribution of resources. These are not distant dreams but attainable goals, guided by the principles we have explored throughout this book.

From Asphalt to Urban Renaissance

The journey through parking lot economics has been one of discovery—revealing hidden networks, uncovering cultural codes, and highlighting the complex interplay of technology, policy, and human behavior. Yet, the lessons extend far beyond the asphalt. They challenge us to rethink our values, reimagine our urban spaces, and reframe our understanding of what it means to live in a modern city.

At its core, parking is a microcosm of urban life—a place where economic imperatives meet cultural expressions, where private interests intersect with public policy, and where individual choices contribute to collective outcomes. The humble parking lot, often overlooked and taken for granted, holds within it the keys to a deeper understanding of urban dynamics. By studying parking, we have gained insights into how we value space, how we interact with our environment, and how our cities can evolve to meet the challenges of the future.

These insights offer a roadmap for a new urban paradigm—one that is more efficient, sustainable, and inclusive. They remind us that every decision we make, from the layout of a parking garage to the policies governing land use, has the power to shape the future of our cities. As we move forward, it is essential that we carry these lessons with us, applying them not only to parking but to every aspect of urban planning and development.

The challenges we face in the 21st century—climate change, urbanization, social inequality, and technological disruption—demand that we think holistically about the spaces we inhabit. By viewing parking as a microcosm of these broader issues, we are better equipped to design solutions that are innovative, resilient, and humane. The future of urban life depends on our ability to understand and manage the complexities of space, value, and behavior—a lesson that begins with something as simple as a parking spot.

As you reflect on your daily routine—whether it involves circling a lot in search of a coveted space or tapping your phone to pay for parking—remember that these seemingly mundane moments are part of a much larger narrative. They are expressions of economic dynamics, cultural values, and social interactions that define our modern world. By paying attention to these details, we can learn to appreciate the hidden networks that drive our urban existence and, in doing so, help create cities that are better places to live.

In closing, the lessons beyond the asphalt are a call to reexamine how we value and use space. They challenge us to look beyond traditional metrics of success—such as profit margins and square footage—and to consider the broader implications of our choices on community well-being, environmental sustainability, and social equity. As cities continue to grow and evolve, the ability to harness these insights will be crucial in shaping a future that is not only prosperous but also vibrant and inclusive.

Let this chapter serve as both a reflection on what we have learned and a call to action.

In the end, the lessons beyond the asphalt are a reminder that every aspect of our built environment has the potential to tell a story—a story of innovation, resilience, and transformation. By understanding and embracing these lessons, we can help shape a future where every parking spot, every street, and every public space contributes to a more sustainable, equitable, and vibrant urban world. The insights derived from the economics of parking have far-reaching implications, offering us a new lens through which to view urban life. It is an invitation to rethink, redesign, and reinvest in our cities—not just for the sake of efficiency, but for the creation of urban environments that reflect the values and aspirations of our time.

Did you love *Under the Asphalt*? Then you should read *The Billionaire Limit*[1] by Jack Donahue!

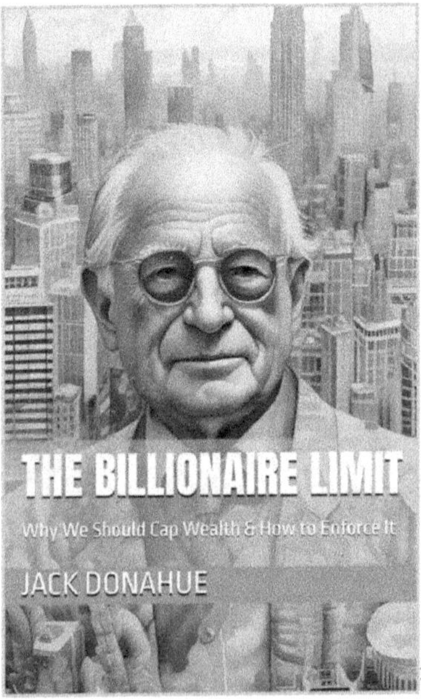

[2]

In the world we live in today, the existence of billionaires is often seen as an inevitable byproduct of capitalism, or worse, as a sign of its success. Wealth accumulation on such a massive scale is frequently celebrated as a reflection of innovation, hard work, and entrepreneurial genius. Business magazines put billionaires on their covers, books are written about how to emulate their achievements, and governments bend over backward to keep them happy. But what if we told a different story—one that challenges the idea that anyone should ever

1. https://books2read.com/u/mdadqw

2. https://books2read.com/u/mdadqw

accumulate a billion-dollar fortune? What if we questioned not just how billionaires are made, but whether billionaires should exist at all?

This book sets out to do exactly that. It challenges the prevailing narrative that extreme wealth is something to be admired or aspired to. It asks readers to consider the moral, economic, and social implications of a world where a handful of people control more wealth than entire nations. In doing so, it invites us to confront some uncomfortable truths about inequality, power, and the structures that allow for such vast disparities of wealth in the first place.

The existence of billionaires is not just a matter of individual success stories. It is a symptom of a system that is deeply imbalanced, where economic growth benefits the few at the expense of the many. When a single person has more wealth than they could ever reasonably use in a lifetime, while millions struggle to afford basic necessities like housing, healthcare, and education, it's clear that something is profoundly wrong.

This book is not simply about decrying billionaires for their wealth. It is about interrogating the systems—economic, political, and cultural—that make such extreme wealth possible. More importantly, it's about exploring what a world without billionaires might look like and how we might get there. It envisions a future where wealth is more equitably distributed, where resources are used to address collective needs rather than personal excess, and where the concentration of wealth no longer threatens the health of our democracies, our economies, and our planet.

We will start by examining why billionaires are a problem—not just in theory, but in practice. From there, we'll dive into how wealth at this scale is accumulated, often through exploitation, monopolistic practices, and tax avoidance. We'll consider the influence billionaires wield over politics, media, and public discourse, and the ways in which this influence erodes democracy itself. Along the way, we'll offer concrete proposals for how society can limit extreme wealth, redistribute resources, and move toward a fairer and more just future.

At the heart of this book is a simple but radical proposition: billionaires shouldn't exist. Not because wealth, in and of itself, is inherently bad, but because no one person should have such an outsized share of the world's resources and power. The cost to society, to democracy, and to the planet is simply too great. And it's not enough to rely on the goodwill of billionaires to solve the world's problems through philanthropy or charity. We need systemic change that addresses the root causes of inequality and prevents such extreme concentrations of wealth from accumulating in the first place.

The journey we are about to take together will ask hard questions about fairness, justice, and the kind of world we want to live in. It will challenge us to rethink the assumptions that have shaped our economies and societies for decades. But ultimately, it will offer hope: hope that a more equal and just world is possible, and that a future without billionaires can be one where prosperity and dignity are shared by all, not hoarded by a few.

Let's imagine a world without billionaires. And let's get to work on building it.

www.ingramcontent.com/pod-product-compliance
Lightning Source LLC
La Vergne TN
LVHW022045200926
848481LV00003B/799

9798230238324